What's Gnu?

What's Gnu?

A HISTORY OF THE CROSSWORD PUZZLE

■ *By Michelle Arnot* ■

VINTAGE BOOKS

A Division of Random House ■ *New York*

Library of Congress Cataloging in Publication Data
Arnot, Michelle.
What's gnu?
1. Crossword puzzles—History.
2. Crossword puzzles. I. Title.
GV1507.C7A76 1981   793.73'2   80–25394
ISBN 0–394–74408–X

Manufactured in the United States of America

Book design: Elissa Ichiyasu

To Roger,
for suggesting I construct
crosswords

■ F O R E W O R D ■

When I was considerably younger and an up-and-coming puzzle expert, I came across this poser in the puzzle section of some magazine: "To double six five hundred add; 'tis very clear, my little lad." I was stumped. Finally I read it to my sister, who had little use for puzzles, and asked if it meant anything to her. She thought a second and then said, "How about VIVID?" My expertise was stained forever, and she never let me hear the end of it.

From that time on I became a closet puzzle solver. I refused to admit or share my weaknesses with anyone. Even now I tend to get flustered if somebody asks my help on a crossword puzzle and I can't come up with the answer. Maybe some other people feel the same way.

However, an attractive and capable young woman named Michelle Arnot, who knows a thing or two about puzzles herself, may have come to our rescue in this book. By giving us an insight into the background and development of various kinds of puzzles, she tends to instill new confidence and familiarity in the field.

Although she leaves the specifics of puzzle technique to other sources, the broad view of the puzzle spectrum that she provides should help make our conversations sparkle and, one hopes, give new impetus to the challenge and enjoyment that puzzles are supposed to provide.

Will Weng

■ A C K N O W L E D G M E N T S ■

The author would like to extend special thanks to those experts who shared a wealth of information on the subject of puzzling. Foremost among these are the late Eugene Sheffer, mentor to the author in the world of crosswords, whose reminiscences inspired this book; Will Shortz, whose expertise in enigmatology past and present gave direction to the research and provided answers to many of the mysteries; and Will Weng, whose good-humored cooperation explained the whimsy associated with the crossword today. She is also grateful to an illustrious list of correspondents for their contributions: Eugene T. Maleska of *The New York Times*, Edmund Akenhead of the London *Times*, Brian Head of the Crossword Club, and such well-known constructors as Thomas H. Middleton, Maura Jacobson, Jack Luzzatto, Emily Cox and Henry Rathvon.

Finally, the author thanks Michael Donner of *Games* magazine, Jo Paquin of King Features Syndicate and Fran Savage of Simon and Schuster for their insights on the evolution of the crossword and its variations, and Nancy Gallt for elucidating the mechanics of the diagramless.

Note: Answers to puzzles may be found on pp. 177–195.

■ C O N T E N T S ■

What's Gnu?

The Ancestors: Riddles, Rebuses, Anagrams, Acrostics and Charades

One of the most universally popular inventions of the twentieth century is the crossword puzzle. Popular demand has ensured that today close to 99 percent of the world's daily newspapers from Bombay and Hong Kong to New York, London, Paris and Rome carry a daily crossword. So do 677 Sunday papers in the United States. During World War II, when the paper shortage became acute, American tabloids tried to drop the crossword puzzle, but anguished protests from fans promptly reinstated it. In Britain, where the shortage was even graver, puzzles had their place in four-page condensed newspapers; they were considered a therapeutic diversion during long hours in air-raid shelters. So pervasive has the crossword puzzle become in our civilization that it is startling to realize that the first one appeared only in 1913. Clearly, it touched some basic human chord, and indeed its ancestors had a long and honorable history.

According to a piece entitled "Antiquity and Dignity of Puzzles," from the 1906 book *Key to Puzzledom*, John Q. Boyer points to the riddle as the earliest known manifestation of the human desire to solve enigmas (Fig. 1). Riddles appear in all cultures. Plutarch and Ovid credit the Sphinx with asking the first one, which was, of course, the famous, "What walks

There is a certain natural production neither animal, vegetable, nor mineral. It generally exists from two to six feet above the surface of the earth. It has neither length, breadth, nor substance. It is neither male nor female, but commonly exists between both. It is often spoken of in the Old Testament, and strongly recommended in the New; and serves equally the purposes of treachery and fidelity.

on four legs in the morning, two legs in the afternoon and three legs in the evening?" which Oedipus correctly answered was Man.

Another famous riddler of antiquity was Samson. Before he succumbed to Delilah, he fell in love with a girl from the Philistine city of Timnath and decided to marry her. In accordance with the custom of the day, the wedding festivities included a special time devoted to riddles. Hoping to provide some amusement while impressing his new in-laws, Samson posed this riddle at the wedding feast: "Out of the eater came forth meat, and out of the strong came forth sweetness." The Bible tells us that he set a seven-day period for solving it and offered a prize of thirty changes of clothing and an equal number of sheets. What Samson had in mind was a striking sight he had passed: bees that were swarming in the carcass of a lion he had killed earlier. The Philistines, unable to guess the riddle, pressured the bride, who elicited the answer from Samson.

After the appointed time elapsed, the group reconvened. Smugly, the Philistines observed: "What is sweeter than honey? And what is stronger than a lion?" Samson proved to be a bad loser. He destroyed their corn-fields, and thousands of Philistines were killed, among them his new wife.

Fortunately, riddling did not often lead to a tragic end. For example, Boyer describes how the Queen of Sheba visited King Solomon expressly to test his legendary aptitude at answering riddles. Solomon had little trouble maintaining his reputation until Hiram, King of Tyre, arrived to challenge him. In an unprecedented match, the two set up a system whereby the loser paid a fine. For several rounds Solomon was the uncon-tested winner. Finally, in desperation, Hiram hired Abdemon, a man known for his skill at solving riddles, and the tables were turned.

To the ancient Greeks, proficiency in riddling was considered a sign of superior schooling. Aristotle attributed the riddle's appeal to the meta-phorical quality of the problem and its answer. Sophism, the method of teaching via a series of questions, was regarded as a form of riddling. Sages often exchanged puzzles to test one another's wits, especially at banquets where enigmatical questions provided the major form of enter-tainment. Cleobulus, one of the Seven Wise Men of Greece, is said to have earned his title with a clever puzzle that for obvious reasons came to be known as "The Year Riddle": "A father had twelve children and each child had thirty sons and daughters, the sons being white and the daughters black, and one of them died every day and yet became immortal."

It has even been suggested that Homer's death may have been precipi-tated by a riddle that the fishermen of Ios posed to him: "What we caught we threw away: what we could not catch we kept." Unable to solve it, Homer allegedly died of chagrin. (The answer is "fleas.")

The Romans further elaborated the riddle. During the religious holiday of Saturnalia in mid-December, riddle-solving was a popular party game. Occasionally, an ambitious gift-giver would devise riddles to describe his presents. Interest in riddling peaked in Nero's reign and waned with the onset of the Christian era. Then in the fourth century A.D. the great riddle-maker Symphosius breathed life back into the art. He composed a series of one hundred short, witty hexameters with giveaway titles:

Mother of Twins
More have I borne than one body ought.
Three souls did I have, all of which I
Had within me: a pair departed,
But the third nearly perished too.

His style gave rise to a host of imitators, most prominently a seventh-century English saint and scholar-poet named Aldhelm, who constructed his work in a religious vein and compiled one hundred of what he felt to be the best examples in a volume called *De Metris*.

Riddles engendered a plethora of word games in different forms, many of which appeared in 1873 in a mysteriously anonymous volume, entitled *The Modern Sphinx*. The book pays tribute to ancient dabblers in the field of wordplay, among them the Theban lyric poet Pindar (whose name appears regularly in crossword puzzles today), who composed an ode that omitted the letter *sigma*. Another Greek poet, Tryphiodorus, took this device a step further. A self-styled lipogrammatist (letter-dropper), he wrote an epic poem about the adventures of Odysseus, a twenty-four volume work in which the letter *alpha* is omitted from the first book, *beta* from the second, and so on down the twenty-four-letter Greek alphabet. The Bible's so-called Abecedarian Psalm (#119) adopted the complementary strategy: each eight-line stanza begins with words whose initials are letters of the Hebrew alphabet in their chronological order (*aleph, beth, gimel,* etc.).

Boyer considers the rebus, a visual puzzle that combines words with pictures, one of the first significant offshoots of the riddle (Fig. 2). The hieroglyphics of Egypt and Phoenicia have been credited as the models for these, but there is no concrete proof to uphold the theory. The rebus has, however, been traced back to at least 600 B.C., to what are known as the Ephesian letters. These magic characters were marked on the crown, belt and feet of representations of the goddess Diana as indications of her powers. Symbolic ideographs of this type were originally guarded by priests, and only a select few had access to the secret knowledge contained in them.

Over the centuries the rebus evolved into a seal used as a form of signature. Ancient Roman rebus coins depict elephants—the Mauritanian translation of the name Caesar. Cicero used a small chickpea (*cicer*) when ending a letter. This stylized pictorial representation was revived in the coats of arms common to the Middle Ages. Heraldic shields encapsulated family history; the crest was the embodiment of achievement through the generations, depicting births, deaths and military conquests.

The rebus achieved its greatest all-time popularity in Picardy in the late sixteenth and early seventeenth centuries. In order to make the Easter

PREFACE.

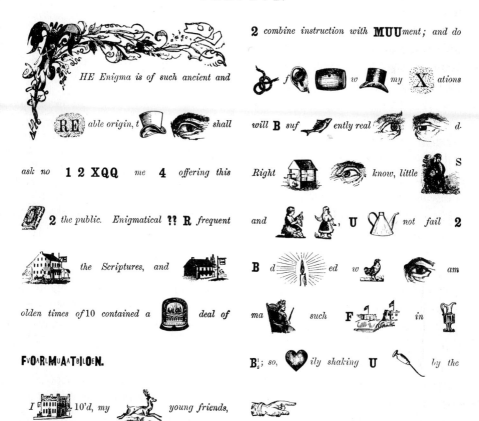

HE Enigma is of such ancient and

RE able origin, t 🎩 eye shall

ask no **1 2 XQQ** me **4** offering this

📖 2 the public. Enigmatical **‽ R** frequent

🏠 the Scriptures, and 🏚

olden times of 10 contained a 🔔 deal of

FVOARLMUAATBILOEN.

I 🏛 10'd, my 🦌 young friends,

2 combine instruction with **MUU**ment; and do

🪢 f 👂 🛢 w 🎩 my ⬛ ations

will **B** suf 🐟 ently real 👁👁 d.

Right 🏠 👁 know, little 👤 **S**

and 🧎 🧍, **U** ⛶ not fail **2**

B d ✴ ed w 🐓 👁 am

ma 🧓 such **F** 🏰 in 🏺

B¹⁄₄; so, ♥ ily shaking **U** 🪈 by the

👉

👁 re 🐴

🏺🏺 truly,

AUNT SUE.

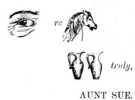

messages accessible to their illiterate parishioners, priests in this region of northern France designed pamphlets that combined words with pictures. They called these tracts *De Rebus Quae Geruntur* (Concerning Things Which Are Accomplished), from which the name derived. The response was more enthusiastic than anyone had anticipated, a trend that seems to characterize puzzle fads through the ages. Rebuses became the rage: Lyons was soon represented by a lion; publishers used clever logos to illustrate their names, such as a pike and a ring to mean Pickering. In *The Alchemist*, Ben Jonson explains the workings and construction of rebuses.

Names offered another source of material for word games. Fascination with the secret power of names began with the Greeks, who called this pastime "anagrams," literally "letters backward." The original object was to read the mirror image of the name as a sort of palindrome. However, this technique limited the possibilities, and so the letters were transposed to create a different word instead; often the new word was regarded as an omen that foretold the future of the person named. Like astrological devices, anagrams were thought to determine character. William Camden, an antiquary who lived in the early seventeenth century (a time known as "the golden age of the anagram"), defines the game as the "dissolution of a name truly written into his letters, as his elements, and a new connection of it, by artificial transposition without addition, subtraction, or change of any letter, into different modes, making some perfect sense to the person named."

Indeed, as Boyer points out, the anagram often led to the choice of avocation. One Carmelite monk, Father Pierre de St. Louis, stumbled into his career when he transposed his lay name into the phrase: "*Carmelo se devouet.*" A more notorious character is André Pujon, whose name was jumbled into "*pendu à Rion.*" (At this time the letters "i" and "j" were interchangeable.) This unfortunate man took it upon himself to fulfill his fate by committing a murder that led to his hanging in Rion (now Riom), the seat of criminal justice in Auvergne.

Lycophron, a poet of the third century B.C., is the first man known to have made a business out of anagrammatizing. As a servant in the court of King Ptolemy Philadelphus of Egypt, he provided amusement by creating satirical anagrams for many of the courtiers. For the royal couple themselves he prudently came up with a pair of flattering transpositions: the king's name became "made of honey," while Queen Arsinoë's name was arranged to read "Hera's violet."

In the thirteenth century A.D., the Jewish cabalists rediscovered the secret powers of anagrams. Believing that the Scriptures contained encoded messages, they used anagrams to decipher the deeper meanings. A well-known example from the cabalist era is presented in *The Modern Sphinx* as a dialogue between Jesus and Pilate:

> Pilate: *Quid est veritas?* (What is truth?)
> Jesus: *Est vir qui adest.* (It is the man before you.)

In the fifteenth and sixteenth centuries, according to Boyer, the use of anagrams spread. Authors in need of anonymity often adopted an anagram of their own name as a handy pseudonym. Calvin's early publications were signed "Alcuinus," in accordance with the anagram rule that V = U. François Rabelais became "Alcofribas Nasier." The eighteenth century provided one of the most famous of all anagrams. A French writer named Arouet, l.j. (*le jeune*) began to sign himself Voltaire. It has since been pointed out that Voltaire can be further anagrammatized to read "*o alte vir*" (O noble man).

An anagram that captured the essence of the person named came to be regarded as the ultimate achievement. Courtiers eager to curry favor spent long hours trying to devise flattering anagrams for their royal masters. In the December 19, 1896 issue of *The Living Age* an article "On Anagrams" included the anagram "*Anglis agria, Hiberiae lea*" made from the Latinized name of Queen Elizabeth I, Elisabetha Regina Angliae. However, this valiant effort is less than perfect, for it omits some letters in the interests of grammar. Another translator, *The Modern Sphinx* informs us, when dedicating his work to James I, the former James Stuart, came up with the witty anagram "a just master." The same sovereign, also known as Charles James Stuart, was further anagrammatized into "claims Arthur's seat," a play on his heritage. On a more sober note, Maria Steuarda Scotorum Regina was posthumously jumbled into "*Trusa vi regnis morte amara cado*" (thrust by force from my kingdom I fall by a foul death).

The fad soon spread from the court to the people. The Huguenots used a bitter anagram of Charles de Valois, "*Va chasser l'Idole*," as the Protestant countersign. This phrase meant death on the eve of the St. Bartholomew massacre, thereby securing the anagram a place in the annals of history.

In an article entitled "The Anagram," also from *Key to Puzzledom*, John L. Hervey discusses the status of the game in America. Perhaps because of the poor communications system in the new nation, very few writers distinguished themselves in this field. Nevertheless, a man known only as "Bolis" created a few that have been preserved. For example, he transformed Miguel de Cervantes Saavedra, the author of *Don Quixote*, into "Gave us a damned clever satire," and Dante Gabriel Rossetti into "greatest born idealist." In England Joseph Addison wrote a satirical piece in which he portrayed a devoted lover who isolated himself for six months with the sole purpose of devising anagrams on his lady's name, only to discover later that he had misspelled it.

Experts agree that despite rebuses, anagrams and riddles, the crossword descends most directly from the word square. In his 1974 book *Crossword Puzzles: Their History and Cult*, Roger Millington names the stele of Moschion as the earliest prototype of the game. This stele, which provides the unusual opportunity to use the common crossword clue "inscribed slab or pillar," is the first known example of a word square. Until the creation of this stele (circa A.D. 300), magical squares consisted mainly of numerical incantations. Moschion, an enterprising Egyptian with a working knowledge of Greek, carved on a slab of alabaster a square that numbered thirty-nine boxes across and down (Fig. 3). Into each of the 1,521 squares, he engraved a Greek letter. To decipher the message, the reader had to begin at the center "o" and continue either up or down, left or right, then turn at the right angle to the next corner. The puzzle could also be read in step sequence by starting at the center "o" and moving in a zigzag fashion one box at a time. The phrase "Moschion to Osiris, for the treatment which cured his foot" repeats in this manner. Evidently, Moschion felt he owed the Egyptian god of the underworld, Osiris, a good turn for his remarkable recovery from a foot ailment. Also inscribed on the stele are poems expressing the pride that Moschion took in this unusual homage to Osiris.

Boyer reports that a similar message can be found at the church of San Salvador in Oviedo, Spain, on the tomb of Prince Silo—a square of nineteen boxes that reads in 270 different ways. Beginning at the central "s" the message reads *"Silo Princeps Fecit"* (Prince Silo made this). Apparently puzzles of this sort are easy to devise from phrases that contain an

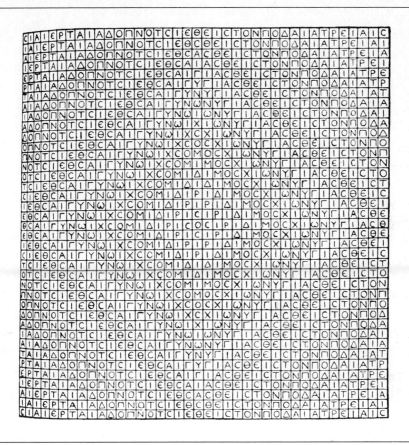

odd number of letters, so perhaps these early constructors were no more than clever magicians who knew enough not to give away the trick.

Millington mentions a variation on the word square known as the "stoicheidon" inscription, which was common to Athens in the sixth century B.C. Although the words were placed within a rectangular frame, they read only horizontally and sometimes ended in midword if the constructor miscalculated; the aesthetic dictates did not require coherence. For the archaeologist, filling in blanks and solving the codes on these engravings represents the same type of accomplishment that a crossword-solver achieves on a particularly good Sunday afternoon.

The Phaestus disc is considered the oldest possible crossword puzzle in existence—but we have yet to find a cryptologist clever enough to fathom its inscrutable hieroglyphics! Discovered on Crete, this mysterious terra-cotta disc dates back to the second century B.C. or earlier, according to an article in the March 1925 issue of *Popular Mechanics*. It bears a spiral inscription on both sides that has thus far remained indecipherable. Perhaps some day a persistent decoder may read it—just as Jean-François Champollion unraveled the message of the Rosetta stone. This four-and-a-half-by-two-foot basalt stone, discovered by one of Napoleon's officers at the Rosetta mouth of the Nile in 1799, posed an enormous riddle to scholars for more than twenty years. Finally, after other experts had paved part of the way, Champollion deduced that, by using the Greek portion of the stone as a guide, the Egyptian code in both demotic and hieroglyphics would be revealed. The three-part decree announced the support by the Memphis priesthood of Ptolemy Epiphanes, ruler of Egypt from 203 to 181 B.C. Champollion first translated the Greek text as a guide. He then began searching for Cleopatra's name in the Egyptian; in addition, he was able to recognize the symbols for "Ptolemy" by using the overlapping letters *p, t, o, l* and *e*. Applying this method to the hieroglyphic section, he assigned values to each ideograph, thereby establishing the basic method by which future archaeologists would decipher this type of inscription.

Millington traces the crossword to the so-called Sator square, first discovered on a piece of wall plaster at the Roman excavation site of Corinium (now Cirencester) in England in 1868. The Sator square was later found in identical form at Pompeii, dating from the time of the eruption of Vesuvius (circa A.D. 79). It reads:

```
R  O  T  A  S
O  P  E  R  A
T  E  N  E  T
A  R  E  P  O
S  A  T  O  R
```

The square is unique in that it translates into two coherent sentences: "The sower Arepo holds the wheels at work" and "Arepo the sower holds the wheels with force"; both of these can be interpreted as statements of the concept that God controls the universe. The square can also be read in any of four different ways: left to right, top to bottom, bottom to top, and right to left. The origin of this well-crafted work has long been a matter of speculation among scholars.

Some sixty years after its original discovery, a German scholar ana-grammed the letters of the word square to read as follows:

```
                        A
                        P
                        A
                        T
                        E
                        R
      A P A T E R N O S T E R O
                        O
                        S
                        T
                        E
                        R
                        O
```

The cross configuration, in addition to the message contained in it ("Our Father, A to O," that is, alpha to omega), seemed to indicate a Christian influence. Scholars suspected that the word square was probably a secret sign used among Christians during times of persecution.

In January 1925 the issue reached the pages of the London *Times*. A Reverend W. Hopkinson proposed that the puzzle be read as a palin-drome—that is, as a mirror image: *Sat orare poten? Et opera rotas.* (Are you able to pray sufficiently? And you gabble through the church services.)

His interpretation was based on an inscription he had spotted in the Church of Great Gidding in England, where he formerly served as vicar. The inscription was dated 1614; he theorized that the remark referred to the incumbent of that era. Two initials had been carved on either side of the square: E. R. With a little research, Hopkinson uncovered the name, that of a certain Edward Rumbolt. In conclusion, he decided that the slur was meant to describe Rumbolt's style of conducting the service.

Hopkinson's opinion sparked conjecture from other ecclesiastical schol-ars, and much correspondence was exchanged on the subject until discov-ery of the original was made at Pompeii in 1936. This new piece of evidence put interpretations with Christian symbolism in question, as the presumed date of the square preceded the arrival of Christianity to that city. Furthermore, the square is written in Latin whereas the early Chris-tians worshiped in Greek. However, it is possible that the square served different purposes at different times. It is believed that it may have been used as a cure for both toothache and fever; some have suggested that it served as an amulet against evil circumstances.

While the shape of the crossword puzzle derives from the word square, the notion of differentiated verticals and horizontals probably derives from the acrostic, a term that is a combination of the Greek *akros* (at the end) and *stichos* (line of verse) (Fig. 4). By reading the initial letters of each line vertically, a key word or phrase related to the subject at hand will emerge. Boyer writes that the sibyls or prophetesses of ancient Greece used acrostics as fortune-telling devices, claiming that they were written on leaves. Cicero mentions the technique in *De Divinatione*: "The verses of the sibyls are distinguished by that arrangement which the Greeks call Acrostic; where from the first letters of each verse in order, words are formed which express some particular meaning; as in the case of Ennius's verses, the initial letters of which make 'which Ennius wrote.' "

Boyer goes on to discuss Eusebius of Caesarea, a fourth-century Greek theologian and church historian, who attributed this immortal acrostic to the Erythraean sibyl:

'Iησους	Jesus
Χριστός	Christ,
θεου	of God,
Υιός	Son,
Σωτηρ	Savior.

The combined first letters spell IXθΥΣ, which means "fish," and accounts for the mystical fish symbol in early Christian art. The Latin equivalent reads INRI (*Iesus Nazarenus, Rex Iudaeorum*), a common inscription often found in paintings of the crucifixion.

The acrostic was rediscovered in the Renaissance, when poets found it particularly suitable for love poems. One lovestruck monk painstakingly composed the lengthy tale of an anonymous brother's devotion to Sister Polia. The initial letters of each section of this work spell out "*Poliam frater Franciscus columna peramavit*" (Brother Franciscus passionately loved Polia). Boccaccio emulated this style in *Amorosa Visione*, where the initial letters of the odd-numbered lines in the first poem reveal the name of his beloved, Maria. And during the Elizabethan age, many English poets fashioned acrostics in honor of the queen. A century and a half later, Addison speculated on the questionable merit of both the anagram and the acrostic, wondering which of the two possessed the least literary value. Of

A valuable ally of family sociability, and what pertains to it.
1. A species of garment.
2. An ancient French coin.
3. One of the Ladrone Islands.
4. An insect.
5. A man's name.

the latter he wrote: "I have seen some of them where the verses have not only been edged by a name at each extremity, but have the same name running down like a seam through the middle of the poem."

Acrostics soon grew to include the telestich, which has vertical words with opposite meanings at both the start and finish of the verse. One of the most famous of these in Millington's estimation is:

Unite and untie are the same—so say yo   U
Not in wedlock, I ween, has this unity bee   N
In the drama of marriage, each wandering ou   T
To a new face would fly—all except you and   I
Each seeking to alter the spell in their scen   E.

With the introduction of movable type, the puzzle came into its own in Victorian England. Magazines and periodicals began to appear with regularity, and through their pages puzzles became available to a wider audience. Until this time, puzzles had possessed a somewhat mystical quality—they were either thought of as the handiwork of sages or kings, or were considered an inferior literary form. But with the revolution in printing, they became an official form of entertainment.

Helene Hovanec, author of *The Puzzler's Paradise* (1978), remarks that in early America riddles and puzzles were relegated to occasional appearances in local almanacs. The first known editor to include such frivolity among the necessary farming information was Samuel Danforth, a Harvard man. In the 1647 edition of his almanac, he added twelve enigmatical verses—one per month—to the usual forecast of the seasons and astrological influences. For July he fashioned this one:

> The wooden Birds are now in sight,
> Whose voices roare, whose wings are white,
> Whose mawes are fill'd with hose and shoes,
> With wine, cloth, sugar, salt and newes.
> When they have eas'd their stomacks here
> They cry, farewell until next yeare.

(The birds are metaphorical allusions to the ships that brought supplies to the American colonists.)

Another illustrious riddler was Benjamin Franklin, who included some in *Poor Richard's Almanac* of 1736. This clever marketing device obliged readers to buy the following edition in order to get the answers.

At this time, puzzles were commonly viewed as female diversions. In 1784, *Boston Magazine* printed a letter to the editor from a woman who wrote:

> I visit in almost every family in town, genteel and vulgar, and from Lady——
> down to Dorothy my maid, every female understanding has been exercised in the
> discovery of those [puzzles] which you have published.

From all this feverish puzzle activity new word games evolved. The most popular was the charade, a term derived from the Portuguese *char-rad(o)* (entertainment) (Fig. 5). This type of riddle divides the answer into its basic components: syllables. Each enigmatical question when solved will reveal the answer piecemeal; once the various parts of the problem are solved and strung together, the complete response appears. For example, this short charade on the word "yellowhammer" from *The Modern Sphinx*:

> My *first* is a color, my *second* a workman's instrument, and my *whole* a pretty little
> bird.

> My *first* belongs, in pairs, to man and beast,
> And of the gifts of harvest not the least;
> The treasures of my *next* no boy of feeling
> Will e'er disgrace his heart or name by stealing;
> My *first* and *third* the time, my *whole* the way
> To undertake the duties of each day.

Key words are represented by numerals to indicate their position in the answer. As the game evolved, clues were soon presented in verse and eventually the game developed into an acting exercise.

In America, *The Penny Post* of Philadelphia led this craze; in England *London Magazine* kept its readers appeased. A most perplexing example of a verse charade was written by the English poet Winthrop Mackworth Praed, who made his reputation with humorous verse. Intentionally or not, he authored this charade without divulging the correct answer; general consensus has agreed that "good (k)night" is probably the most appropriate response:

> Sir Hilary charged at Agincourt;
> Sooth, 'twas an awful day!
> And though in that old age of sport
> The rufflers of the camp and court
> Had little time to pray,
> 'Tis said Sir Hilary muttered there
> Two syllables by way of prayer:

My *First* to all the brave and proud
 Who see to-morrow's sun:
My *Next*, with her cold and quiet cloud,
To those who find their dewy shroud
 Before today's be done:
And both together to all blue eyes
That weep when a warrior nobly dies.

The charade fad caught on quickly, and easily dominated the puzzle world. Even the *Encyclopaedia Britannica* included the word: " . . . charades, if not greatly constructive, is at least innocent and amusing. At all events, as it has made its way into every fashionable circle, it will scarcely be deemed unworthy of attention." The demand for puzzles appeared insatiable; in fact, it has never ceased since its boom in popularity in the Victorian era.

One of the next puzzles to sweep the English-speaking population was the double acrostic, an improved version of the acrostic verse trick and one of the forerunners of the present Double-Crostic. Rumor has it that Queen Victoria was among the inventors of this clever variation. Apparently she set aside some time from her official duties in order to write a contribution to an impressive volume entitled *Victorian Enigmas; or Windsor Fireside Researches: being a Series of Acrostics Enigmatically Propounded (1861)*. The work, presumed to be by her royal hand, and which came to be known as "The Windsor," reads:

Clues

1. A city in Italy;	N	aple	S
2. A river in Germany;	E	lb	E
3. A town in the U.S.;	W	ashingto	N
4. A town in North America;	C	incinnat	I
5. A town in Holland;	A	msterda	M
6. The Turkish name for Constantinople;	S	tambou	L
7. A town in Bothnia;	T	orne	A
8. A city in Greece;	L	epant	O
9. A circle on the globe.	E	clipti	C

Prince Albert is suspected of helping his wife with this puzzle. According to *The Modern Sphinx*, the royal couple were reputed to be "more than ordinarily clever in constructing this sort of riddle."

As eager solvers sought more challenging horizons, new word games were created to order. The *dernier cri* became letter manipulation: a method of adjusting a word by one letter to create another "hidden" word. A whole science evolved from this type of puzzle, which came to be known as logographs or logogriphs. Each variation was assigned a deceptively sober-sounding title. Beheadment indicates the loss of the initial letter to create a new word, as in the following example:

> Take away one letter and I murder; take away two and I am dying, if the whole does not save me. (Answer: Skill).

Curtailment applied the same type of surgery to the final letter of the word in order to spell another word.

Transpositions are a type of anagram in which the letters of the original word are jumbled to form a different one; both terms are then usually described in a short verse, as in this case:

> Part of a foot with good judgment transpose,
> And the answer you'll find just under your nose. (Answer: Inch/Chin).

Conundrums are riddles that elicit a pun-filled answer. One of the best-known conundrums appears in *The Modern Sphinx*:

> Why is the Prince of Wales like a gorilla, like a bald man and like an orphan?

> Because the Prince is the heir-apparent, the gorilla is a hairy parent, the bald man has no hair apparent, and the orphan has ne'er a parent.

Enigmas are merely sophisticated riddles that are resolved in a straightforward manner, alluding to the answer only by veiled references. Jean-Jacques Rousseau tried his hand at the enigma, using the word "portrait" as inspiration:

> Art's offspring, whom Nature delights here to foster,
> Can Death's dart defy, though not lengthen life's stage.
> Most correct at the moment when most an imposter,
> Still freshening in youth as advancing age.*

These innovations altered puzzles visibly, bringing the actual puzzle rather than its literary aspects to the fore. Replacing esoteric stanzas were clever rhymes—and a new emphasis on prose. This attracted an ever-growing audience; magazine editors compiled the overflow of contributions into books. At first these were privately published for the exclusive pleasure of a few good friends and close relations, but by the end of the nineteenth century, puzzle books were flooding the market.

*From *The Modern Sphinx*, translated by Mrs. Piozzi.

In the last quarter of the nineteenth century, a new audience was recruited: children. Juvenile magazines enjoyed a bustling correspondence with young solvers who submitted their answers in exchange for honorable mention in the puzzle column. *St. Nicholas*, perhaps the most famous of all American children's magazines, featured a column called "The Riddle-Box," which proved to be a source of inspiration for many future puzzle writers (Fig. 6).

In his reminiscence "When Puzzledom Was Young," which appeared in *The Enigma* in August 1928, John L. Hervey ("Majolica") described the preoccupations of childhood in the 1880's, when diversions were exclusively homemade. Young people with intellectual pretensions often became greatly involved with the puzzle departments of the various magazines. Despite the relatively prohibitive cost of postage, these youthful enthusiasts managed to maintain a lengthy correspondence among themselves. Such puzzle-oriented cliques usually included at least one proud owner of an amateur printing kit obtained through a mail-order house. From these miniature presses arose the custom of exchanging "personal cards"—a variation on the adult calling card—which these enterprising businessmen and women printed for a modest fee (25¢ per 100). However, rather than going by their real names, *noms de plume* were adopted. Young puzzle buffs swapped cards and developed reputations based on their pseudonyms.

The first publication to endorse this idea was *Our Boys and Girls*, whose editor, William T. Adams, preferred to be called Oliver Optic. *St. Nicholas* followed suit by adding this note: "To our puzzlers: In sending answers to puzzles, sign only your initials or use a short assumed name." The mystical spirit of the puzzle fraternity continued to preserve its code of secrecy later, with adult constructors retaining pen names.

The Reverend Charles L. Dodgson, who used the pseudonym Lewis Carroll, enjoyed dashing off puzzles to his youthful correspondents and decided to make these works accessible to all such readers. At one point he even considered issuing a small collection of these works with the tentative title *Alice's Puzzle Book*, as a sequel to his best sellers. Although this project never came to pass, he did have a column in the December 1870 issue of *Aunt Judy's Magazine* entitled "Puzzles from Wonderland." Among his best anagrams is that on the name of Florence Nightingale: *Flit on, cheering angel*. He also invented a game called "Doublets" whereby the solver tries to get from one word to another of equal length by altering

THE RIDDLE-BOX.

PROVERB REBUS.

The proverb should be borne in mind when filling Christmas bags.

CONCEALED BIRDS.

1. "IS THERE a glen on your estate, Reginald?" 2. He travels both day and night; in gale and in sunshine. 3. "If the baby is asleep, lay her on the bed." 4. James wanted to go fishing last Friday. 5. "How can you call Ralph awkward?" 6. With encouragement, she would be an excellent pianist. 7. Henry IV. of France was a popular king. 8. The house was flaming on all sides. 9. "Your fine fowls have all gone to roost, Richard." 10. "Oh, Fernando, do not frighten my birds!" 11. Place the red over the gray, to form a pleasing contrast. 12. "Fill the pipe with bark of willow." 13. "Faint the hollow murmur rings, o'er meadow, lake, and stream." 14. "'Tis the break of day and we must away."

L. T. S.

CROSS-WORD ENIGMA.

My first is in call, but not in hear;
My second in doe, but not in deer;
My third is in fowl, but not in bird;
My fourth is in sheep, but not in herd;
My fifth is in earl, but not in king;
My sixth is in whirl, but not in swing.
And my whole—you surely ought to know it—
Is the name of a famous English poet.   MAUD.

A DICKENS DOUBLE ACROSTIC.

For older Puzzlers.

ALL the characters referred to are to be found in Charles Dickens's novels.

PRIMALS: A retired army officer who boasts of being "Tough, sir!"
FINALS: A schoolboy, addicted to drawing skeletons.
CROSS-WORDS: 1. The surname of a woman who apparently spends all her time washing greens. 2. A name sometimes used in derision of Mrs. Cruncher by her husband. 3. The Christian name of a shy young girl, whom Mr. Lammle tries to induce "Fascination Fledgeby" to marry. 4. The surname of a friend of Mr. Guppy's, who, contrary to the proverb, does not "grow apace." 5. The surname of an eccentric old lady with a great dislike for donkeys. 6. The nickname given to the father of Herbert Pocket's wife. 7. The surname of a genial old fellow, who, having lost his right hand, used a hook in its place. 8. The name of an interesting family who lodged in the house with Newman Noggs.
W.

NUMERICAL OMISSIONS.

MY whole is composed of eleven letters and is a garden cress. Omit 1-2-3-4-5-6 and leave herbage. Omit 7-8-9-10-11 and leave a spice.
W. H.

THREE EASY DIAMONDS.

I. 1. ALWAYS in doubt. 2. Part of a wheel. 3. A city of northern Italy. 4. Large. 5. In tone.
II. 1. In panther. 2. An intelligent animal. 3. A kind of quadruped, noted for its keen sense of smell. 4. An animal that is seldom called "old," no matter how great its age may be. 5. In badger.
III. 1. In lawsuits. 2. A useful animal. 3. A name borne by many kings of France. 4. Sense. 5. In stall.
P + X.

---

only a single letter. One example of this sequence reaches from head to tail in the following manner: *Head/ Heal/ Teal/ Tell/ Tall/ Tail.*

Outstanding among early puzzle constructors were the friendly rivals Samuel Loyd, "Prince of Puzzle Makers in America," and Henry E. Dudeney, who reigned in England. Loyd's skills were honored in *Scientific American*'s November 1971 issue in an article by Martin Gardner, who lauded him as "the most prolific creator of mathematical premiums" (promotional pieces). A student of engineering, Loyd abandoned his profession as soon as he discovered that he could actually earn a living by pursuing his first love: puzzle-making. By devising promotional give-aways, he marketed his skills for advertising purposes; at the same time, he attracted quite a substantial following. His first coup was a device that he designed as an advertising gimmick for P. T. Barnum's circus in 1858, when he was only seventeen. Entitled "Trick Donkeys," the object was to arrange the puzzle so that each rider mounted a donkey. Although the game appeared easy, few could master it, and in later years Loyd revealed that Barnum often returned for a quick refresher in how to solve it (Fig. 7).

Loyd's most spectacular creation—and his own personal favorite—was known as the "Get-Off-the-Earth Puzzle" (Fig. 8). Originally designed in 1896 as an advertisement for Bergen Beach in New Jersey, the puzzle attracted enormous attention and also stirred up considerable controversy. The device consisted of two concentric circles of cardboard designed as globes and fastened by a central rivet to a cardboard rectangle. A tab attached to one disc allowed it to move up and down and rotate in two positions. The circles were bordered by thirteen paper figures of Chinese men in warlike positions. If moved correctly, the number of warriors decreased magically by one. Although the puzzle appeared simple, not one of Loyd's fans was able to explain the disappearance of the thirteenth warrior.

The name of the puzzle, "Get Off the Earth," was meant to refer to the elusive thirteenth Chinese warrior. Unfortunately, the puzzle's appearance coincided with the "yellow peril" scare of the 1890's and American resistance to Oriental immigration. Although Loyd's puzzle could have been misinterpreted as a racial slur, political overtones were overshadowed by the puzzle's inscrutability. For a whole year Loyd kept his fans in suspense. His column in *The Brooklyn Daily Eagle* was deluged with letters from readers with possible solutions—yet no one came up with the answer he had in mind. How did he produce this trompe l'oeil? In accordance with the magician's code of secrecy, he cryptically explained the mechanics behind the masterwork. Apparently, the grotesque quality of the figures, combined with the necessary legerdemain feat of changing a right leg for a left one between two of the men, achieved the desired effect. The smaller inner circle was responsible for this transformation. Even with this hint, the actual mechanics of the trick remain mystifying.

A 1926 interview in the *Strand* reveals that, like Loyd, Dudeney fell into his profession by accident. As a journalist, he occasionally contributed puzzles to *Strand*'s "Tit-bits" column under the signature "Sphinx." His work became so popular that he was soon recruited to work at it full time. Before long he was a permanent fixture in the *Strand* with his "Perplexities" column.

Dudeney regarded puzzle-solving as an intellectual process of the high-

F I G U R E 7 ▪ *"Trick Donkeys," one of Loyd's first commercial efforts, challenged the solver to fold the puzzle in such a way that each rider ends up astride a donkey.*

est type; no one, he claimed, could be more clear-thinking and logical than one who constructed such works. In the 1890's he announced his intention of devoting himself entirely to the invention of problems. He then pioneered new roads by applying scientific principles to his puzzles.

During his efforts to encourage puzzle evolution, Dudeney unwittingly contributed to the evolution of what would become the crossword puzzle. His innovation was the word square complete with clues. An example that dates from 1890 reads:

The Abbey

'Twas spring. The abbey woods were decked with *second*.
The abbot, with his *fifth*, no trouble reckoned;
But shared his meats and *seventh* which every man
Who loves to feast has *first* since time began.
Then comes a stealthy *sixth* across the wall,
Who *fourths* the plate and jewels, cash and all,
And ere the abbot and the monks have dined;
He *thirds*, and leaves no trace or clue behind.

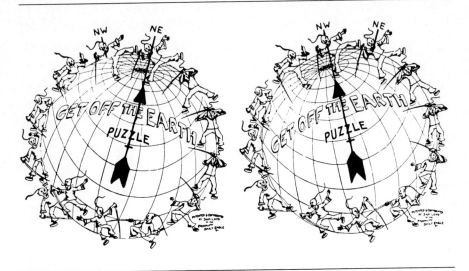

Each numeral should be replaced by the appropriate terms which, when listed in order, form this word square:

```
P A L A T E D
A N E M O N E
L E V A N T S
A M A S S E S
T O N S U R E
E N T E R E R
D E S S E R T
```

After Loyd's death in 1911, Dudeney reigned supreme, unique in his pursuit of the advancement of puzzledom. His enormous correspondence reached its zenith during World War I, when soldiers often placed bets on solutions and then addressed their queries to Dudeney in order to settle those wagers before they were sent to the trenches.

As the ranks of puzzle-solvers swelled, it was simply a matter of time before a society was established to accommodate these eager fans. According to Lewis Trent, one-time secretary of the National Puzzlers' League, the movement began on July 4, 1883 when thirty-four young men convened at the aptly named Pythagoras Hall in New York City. From this meeting emerged the Eastern Puzzlers' League, a fraternity of puzzlers living east of the Mississippi. If any member dared to move too far west, he was automatically dropped.

These intrepid men sought to promote the art of puzzling under the aegis of Armachis, the Egyptian goddess. In her incarnation as the sphinx, Armachis posed enigmas to the Egyptians, who considered their solution a religious ritual. Unlike the bloodthirsty sphinx of the Oedipus myth, the sphinx of Egypt symbolized the higher aspirations of the puzzle craft. Following this example, the Eastern Puzzlers' League resolved to standardize rules and meet twice yearly to cultivate the art of the puzzle.

Three aims were agreed upon: (1) to provide a delightful pastime of mental relaxation for puzzle lovers; (2) to raise the intellectual standard of puzzling; (3) to establish friendships among the members. Members were quoted as expressing such optimistic thoughts as: "Puzzling promises to become the national intellectual pastime of America," and "The mission of Puzzledom is to teach." In 1889, "Planet" (the president of the League at that time) announced: "The distinctiveness of American puzzledom lies not in the subject of which it treats, but in the . . . community of interest which has resulted."

Most significantly, the members agreed to invest their dues in a newsletter that would unite the members and allow for written discussion of the art. This later developed into a monthly, *The Eastern Enigma*, which provided a creative outlet for the puzzlers. Concern focused on the state of the craft rather than personal glory; these dedicated men, who signed their work with *noms de plume*, were determined to upgrade quality.

Rules were considered in order since puzzling "as conducted by our League . . . is fundamentally a form of competition between puzzle maker and puzzle solver." The first action was to limit the number of definitive reference books to the three that were deemed most worthy: a standard dictionary, Phillips's *Dictionary of Biographical Reference*, and Lippincott's *Gazetteer of the World*. Constructors were thereafter required to use these prescribed works; since clues then were straightforward definitions, the solver could easily check his answers by consulting the three reference works.

To standardize the craft further, the League created three general categories: cryptograms, flats and forms. Cryptograms were substitutions of letters for other letters in the style of a secret code; by studying the puzzle, the solver should eventually be able to replace the hidden letters and decipher the message—much as Champollion did with the texts of the Rosetta stone. A flat was a word puzzle presented in verse that was resolved by a single flat row of letters: a word, phrase or sentence. This included anagrams, charades, logogriphs, enigmas and rebuses. Although the acrostic contained vertical answers, it still qualified as a flat because the clues were generally written in verse and the final outcome was usually a word.

Forms were easily recognized by their geometrical shapes; the words dovetailed throughout the length of the puzzle, leaving no blanks. The formist was not limited to the three standard reference works but could consult any work in the English language. The object was to connect as many words as would read identically both vertically and horizontally; one expert noted that only biographical and geographical terms should be used here. The most popular shapes were the pyramid; the diamond, which used odd-numbered words; and the square. (Even more familiar-looking today is the double square, which reads differently in the across and down entries.) A good memory was an asset, since the same words were often repeated, and the definitions were taken from the source without being changed.

As the E.P.L. sought to consolidate puzzlers on the East Coast, other groups sprang up independently. One of the more prestigious was located in New Jersey and was responsible for the short-lived *Newark Puzzler* (1881–84). In Connecticut, the *Mystic Knight* magazine appeared in the late 1870's and folded in the early eighties. The first magazine to feature puzzles exclusively was the product of a small outpost in Auburn, Maine; it made its début in January 1875 and lasted only through the year.

The Eastern Enigma, however, forged ahead in a continuing effort to attract new recruits. By the early 1920's the name had been modified to *The Enigma*, and the Eastern Puzzlers' League had become the National Puzzlers' League, and welcomed members from all over the country. Women members were also now officially accepted, although as it happened many who had adopted ambiguous pseudonyms had already infiltrated the ranks. The most notorious of these was Rayle Rhoder (Mrs. Blanche A. Wheatley, of Harpers Ferry, Virginia). Although she became involved in the puzzle fraternity after women were officially welcomed, the editors took her for a man and she enjoyed the disguise. For five years general consensus believed Rayle Rhoder to be a reclusive, tobacco-chewing mountaineer living somewhere in the Blue Ridge Mountains with only a dog for company. Working on this premise, the editors at *The Enigma* persuaded Rayle Rhoder to become a contributor to a circulating letter called *The Quill*. The other contributors, curious about the new member, began to address direct questions—with little result. Mrs. Wheatley's identity was finally revealed in a 1930 *Enigma* portrait. The *Quill* faction was embarrassed, the article explained, since "we occasionally indulged in quips that we should not have voiced in mixed company." However, Mrs. Wheatley was welcomed after her "glorious masquerade" and heralded as a master of puzzledom who "put it over on a bunch of puzzlers—folks who were supposed to be expert at the game of unraveling mysteries."

By the onset of the twentieth century, the puzzle habit was well-ingrained in American culture. The amount of time spent musing over various word games became a topic of study and even concern. A magazine of the day, *Current Literature*, picked up a scoop from the *Philadelphia Press* in a July 1901 issue. The topic of discussion was the "puzzle brain." Apparently, a bachelor had taken his life in a local hotel when he was unable to solve an undisclosed type of puzzle. Hundreds of upstanding citizens were devoting almost all their leisure time to the puzzle habit. The danger lay in the possibility of losing one's priorities to such a degree that puzzling took precedence over the ordinary business of life; these "alienists" would become obsessed by the game and eventually withdraw from all contact with others. One might even become a "puzzle fiend" if proper measures were not taken.

A celebrated "mind-specialist" was consulted on the matter. "In the pursuit of puzzles, the cranks lead and the sane follow," he is quoted as saying. "It is a morbid taste. The mind of the person who is fond of puzzles is the cynical mind, or a mind that is continually working in circles inside of circles." He goes on to point out that a healthy person who simply enjoys puzzles for amusement will come to no psychological harm. "But if a mental screw gets loose and his mind loses its residual balance, then the passion for puzzles is apt to become abnormal." What he finds most shocking is that some men prefer solving puzzles to an evening at the theater or a thorough reading of the newspaper. He ends with a warning: "I should not say that puzzles are dangerous to children, if they have a liking for them and that liking is kept within bounds. But I should prefer to see my child show a fondness for something else."

All the symptoms were becoming familiar: the loss of interest in daily affairs, the faraway gaze, the compulsion to work puzzle after puzzle. Yet not even the puzzle experts anticipated the scope of the contagion or the proportions it would reach after the development of the crossword puzzle as we now know it.

■ TWO ■

The Birth of the Crossword Puzzle

In 1913, Arthur Wynne, the editor of the "Fun" supplement of *The New York Sunday World*, was determined to feature something new and special in the Christmas issue. The enigmas, riddles, rebuses and anagrams that dominated the eight-page section were beginning to seem dated; readers had been doing them for years. Surely he could come up with something fresher. Born and brought up in Liverpool, England, Wynne had been raised on the ingenious creations of the "Riddle-Box" column in *St. Nicholas* magazine and the puzzles of Henry E. Dudeney. Geometric shapes built from words appealed to him especially; years later, one of his colleagues on the paper, Victor Lawn, recalled a puzzle in *The London Graphic* that had captured Wynne's fancy and that Lawn believed responsible for his subsequent brainstorm.

After looking through all the old magazines he could find for inspiration, Wynne set to work. Synthesizing his research, he decided on a diamond-shaped grid that would read differently across and down; this strategy eliminated the chore of working out a word square that read the same in both directions. Within the diamond he carved out a smaller blank area of the same shape. Then he began the task of filling in the blanks. After hours of doodling, he compiled a viable list, worked out the clues and inserted numbers in the corresponding boxes; each word had two numbers indicating its beginning and end. Below the puzzle he jotted the simple instruction: "Fill in the small squares with words which agree with the following definitions." At the top he scrawled the title "Word-Cross" (probably borrowed from the acrostic clue system) and sent it to the printers (Fig. 9).

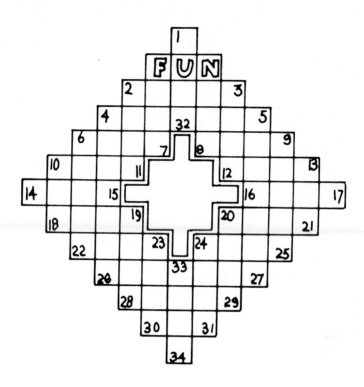

2–3. What bargain hunters enjoy.

4–5. A written acknowledgment.

6–7. Such and nothing more.

10–11. A bird.

14–15. Opposed to less.

18–19. What this puzzle is.

22–23. An animal of prey.

26–27. The close of a day.

28–29. To elude.

30–31. The plural of is.

8–9. To cultivate.

12–13. A bar of wood or iron.

16–17. What artists learn to do.

20–21. Fastened.

24–25. Found on the seashore.

10–18. The fibre of the gomuti palm.

6–22. What we all should be.

4–26. A day dream.

2–11. A talon.

19–28. A pigeon.

F–7. Part of your head.

23–30. A river in Russia.

1–32. To govern.

33–34. An aromatic plant.

N–8. A fist.

24–31. To agree with.

3–12. Part of a ship.

20–29. One.

5–27. Exchanging.

9–25. Sunk in mud.

13–21. A boy.

Except for vociferous complaints from the typesetters, no fanfare marked the debut of Word-Cross. Wynne himself saw it as simply one more contribution to the section, and his colleagues considered it a silly game that provided yet another bothersome detail in the already complicated process of putting out a newspaper. Eleven years later, one *World* editor recalled that the staff regarded the game as "beneath a sensible man's consideration."

Word-Cross appeared on December 21, and to everyone's surprise, it evoked an immediate and positive response from the readers. The little diamond grid charmed a small contingent, who at once began to write letters to the paper about it. The response was sufficient to warrant a second Word-Cross the following Sunday.

The New Year's puzzle came out on December 28 accompanied by a laconic message from Wynne: "The great interest shown in 'Fun's' word-cross puzzle has prompted the puzzle editor to submit another of the same kind." The second puzzle was given more room, to the dismay of the typesetters; in subsequent issues, the clues were set in agate—the smallest possible typeface. By mid-January, the puzzle's name had been transposed to "Cross-Word," perhaps because the subtitle read "Find the missing cross words."

On February 1, the puzzle appeared with this comment: " 'Fun's' cross-word puzzles apparently are getting more popular than ever. The puzzle editor has received from readers many interesting new cross-word puzzles, which he will be glad to use from time to time. It is more difficult to make up a cross-word puzzle than it is to solve one. If you doubt this, try to make one yourself." Perhaps Wynne hoped the note would elicit contributions and relieve him of a weekly responsibility. If so, it succeeded beyond all expectation. On February 8, 1914, when her work was published, Mrs. M. B. Wood of New York City became the first cross-word puzzle contributor in history.

In the months that followed, Wynne was inundated with diagrams inspired by his brief message; from Montreal to Virginia to Wisconsin, readers sent in their efforts. And each contributor was eager to outdo his predecessors in ingenuity. The March 15 entry (already number thirteen!) introduced a new concept: the constructor, a Mr. Harry Cleaver of Montreal, took advantage of the central blank by creating within it a separate puzzle—hence his title, "Two-in-One" (see Fig. 10). Shortly thereafter, Wynne was forced to write, "So many 'Fun' puzzle solvers are sending in cross-word puzzles, made by themselves, with a request that they be published, that the puzzle editor is beginning to wonder what to do with them all. Those puzzles which are available will be published as early as possible."

By April, the constructors were growing more fanciful, elaborating on the original grid in imaginative ways. The Easter Puzzle appeared in the form of a Maltese cross; later puzzles assumed X-shapes and even more intricate rhomboidal designs (Fig. 11). Another innovation, "The Uncompleted Cross-Word," was introduced in July. Instead of this puzzle being solved in the usual manner, several answers were provided. The object here was to fill in the blanks to form a coherent cross-word. To be on the safe side, the editor had already worked out a practicable answer grid so as to be sure of one possible combination. He supplied only this clue: "Just think of a house with [the] furniture, fittings and supplies you will find in a house. With this clue to work on, you can readily call to mind nearly all the words needed to complete the puzzle." This strategy seems like another sly effort on Wynne's part to encourage participation and bow out of construction altogether.

With every contribution featured in "Fun," the constructor added a word of appreciation to the editor. "The solving of your crosswords has been a source of keen delight, not only to myself, but to various members of my family and friends," wrote William Callandar of Brooklyn. Another Brooklyn man explained, "The pleasure I have found in solving the cross-word puzzle in 'Fun' has prompted me to construct the enclosed."

The spreading fame of the cross-word was temporarily halted when war broke out in Europe in 1914. The August papers were filled with maps depicting the aggressive movement of troops and charts of foreign flags for handy reference. But even as the concerned populace followed the grim progress of the war, they never ceased to look forward to the cross-word puzzle, which appeared sporadically during the next few years.

As the puzzle continued to serve as an experimental test of wits to intrepid constructors, Wynne began to take certain liberties. Asserting his position as editor, he no longer printed puzzles as they were submitted but altered them to suit his taste. The first step in this direction occurred in the thirty-seventh puzzle (September 13, 1914). The work of a Mr. E. B. Rust of Yonkers was featured on this date, accompanied by what had become a standard expression of thanks ("Just to show you our appreciation . . . "). In response, Wynne added a tactful editorial note confirming the excellent quality of the contribution but explaining that, in the interest of the constructor, he had changed a few of the entries. "If the puzzle editor of 'Fun'

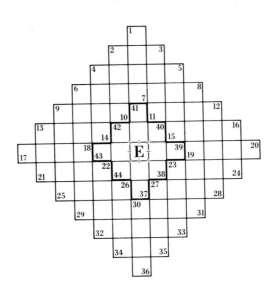

M A I N   D I A M O N D

P U Z Z L E

2–3 Did ᶜeat.*

4–5 Sour substances.

6–8 A continent.

9–10 Beverages.

11–12 Part of a book.

13–14 To paint in water colors.

15–16 High.

17–18 Short for Dorothy.

19–20 To work.

21–22 To watch over.

23–24 To dry with a cloth.

25–26 A raised platform.

27–28 To rescue.

29–31 Blame.

32–33 One who receives a gift.

34–35 Humor.

6–29 A register of the year.

9–25 When dried.

13–21 A piece of land.

3–11 To prepare for publication.

5–15 A native of Scotland.

8–31 Disposed to love.

12–28 To run away to wed.

16–24 An untruth.

22–32 Die—past participle.

26–34 It falls in flakes.

30–36 To cut off.

27–35 Hard fat.

23–33 Merchandise.

1–7 To rouse.

2–10 Highest cards.

4–14 An expression of approval.

*The floating "c" was characteristic of the sloppy typesetting of the early puzzles.

INSIDE DIAMOND PUZZLE

E to 37 Series of years.
E to 38 A tree.
E to 39 Adam's mate.

40 to E To be sorry for.
41 to E Frozen water.
42 to E Used in billiards.
43 to E Used for chopping.
E to 44 A contraction of even.
Starting from 37 and going around to 44 you will find what President Wilson is.

2–3 Plural personal pronoun.
4–5 Opposite of off.
6–7 A conjunction.
8–9 Meaning everything.
10–11 A bright color.
12–13 Space of time.
14–15 A man's favorite room.
16–17 Possessive masculine pronoun.
18–19 The end.
20–21 An object of praise.
22–23 What school children do.
24–25 A children's pet.
26–27 A machinery term meaning rough edges.
28–29 A proper name.
30–32 An abbreviation of a boy's name.
33–34 A metal that shines.
35–36 A summed [typo for summer] month.
37–39 An important organ of the body.
40–41 What many men are.
42–43 What farmers do in spring.
44–45 The fruit of the cedar.
46–49 What water often becomes.
50–51 A golfing term.
52–55 A wicked thing to [do.]
[their typo: misplacing last word of above clue]
56–57 Food for animals.
58–60 2 and 2 are
61–62 A kind of vase.
63–66 A man who handles money.
67–68 Keeps you warm in winter.
69–71 Important part of a sailboat.
72–73 A measure of quantity.
74–75 A little animal.
76–77 To separate into classes.
78–80 It rests you.
81–82 A title of respect in addressing a sovereign.
83–84 A kind of cabbage.
85–87 The first numeral.
88–91 The end.

1–5 A number.
2–11 Where we live.
6–15 A small city in Western New York.
8–19 What a policeman does.
12–23 A famous inventor.
16–25 Boy's first name.
18–27 What the tower of Pisa does.
20–29 A boy's name.
22–34 How some animals catch their prey.
24–39 Boilers do sometimes.
26–38 A wild animal in Germany.
28–52 To build fires in.
33–47 Determined.
37–46 Possesses.
48–53 In contact with.
49–54 What you may call your mother.
55–58 To exist.
30–45 To govern.
31–41 Opposite to young.
32–36 Next to.
35–51 A girl's name.
40–57 Babies are.
50–64 A boy's name.
44–60 Something that gives heat.
[typo: the two clues above should be in reverse positions]
56–68 What a fire does.
59–73 A measure of quantity larger than 72–73
[63–77 omitted]
67–82 Something to beware of.
72–87 A passage for perspiration.
76–86 Something very wicked.
81–85 In like manner.
65–69 A measure of type.
66–74 A small animal women fear.
70–78 A wireless call.
71–83 How we express ourselves.
75–88 An awful affliction.
79–89 A proper name used for a college.
80–90 What we write with.

were to publish it exactly as it was sent in, Mr. Rust would not have any cross-word puzzle to solve this week. So the puzzle editor has taken the great liberty of changing one or two words in order that he too can have an interesting hour or so solving his own puzzle." This thoughtful action established the long tradition of the puzzle editor, whose job it is to tailor each selection for a discerning public (often to the chagrin of the constructor eager to see his or her magnum opus intact).

The forty-first puzzle (October 11) was created by a schoolgirl, who wrote:

Dear Mr. Editor:

Instead of giving us a spelling lesson to study for yesterday, the teacher told us to compose a cross-word puzzle and another girl and I were the only ones in the class who had ours perfect. I enclose mine so that your readers will have some fun working it out.

> Yours truly,
> Della Sherry
> 354 West Seventy-eighth Street,
> New York City.

Wynne published the entire letter to emphasize the educational value of the cross-word (Fig. 12).

From the very first puzzle, correspondence to the puzzle editor was copious and inventive. "You are too easy on the public," wrote J. C. O'Connor of West 86th Street in New York City on November 8, 1914. He thereupon began a one-man campaign to reverse this policy. Two of his high-powered contributions were printed in one month. Mr. O'Connor helped to promote the "Two-in-One" variety of puzzle whereby the entire grid was used (Fig. 13).

There was no celebration for the cross-word's first birthday. The main concern at *The World* was the war in Europe, and had it not been for the many enthusiastic readers the cross-word might have become another war casualty. However, newspapermen are also businessmen, and as long as the puzzle attracted a regular following, it continued to appear despite unending objections from the typesetters. The *World* staff regarded it as a necessary nuisance, which perhaps accounts for the fact that other newspapers did not start their own puzzles.

It was the solvers who shaped the cross-word by sending in constant suggestions, almost all of which were put to practical use. Rules began to emerge; as they were tested, each one was refined to conform to popular taste. First of all, there was an almost universal objection to such devices

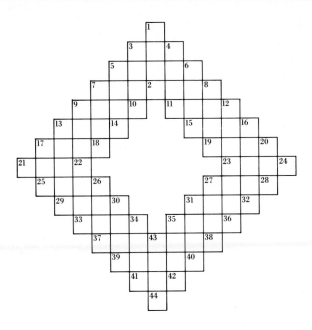

1–2 A mountain top.

3–4 To supplicate.

5–6 What noises generally are.

7–8 Popular at Thanksgiving.

9–10 It comes before Easter.

11–12 Twelve months.

13–14 What Patti did.

15–16 A kingdom in Southeast Asia.

17–18 Despatched.

19–20 Prescribed food.

21–22 Saucy.

23–24 What eggs are.

25–26 Before Thanksgiving and Christmas.

27–28 Needed on washday.

29–30 An eagle.

31–32 What the best man generally does.

33–34 Short sleeps.

35–36 A heavy blow.

37–38 One who plays the piano.

39–40 A woven fabric.

41–42 Part of the foot.

3–10 A boy's name.

4–11 Black and white mixed.

5–14 Suspended.

6–15 Used for coloring goods.

7–18 A canvas shelter.

8–19 Spoken.

9–33 A night light.

12–36 A fence.

13–29 What the waiter does.

16–32 What we all should have.

17–25 To perceive.

20–28 To fasten.

26–37 A sudden breaking.

27–38 Scrapings from linen.

30–39 A narrative poem of elevated style.

31–40 To cleanse with water.

34–41 Chloride of sodium.

35–42 What vicious dogs do.

43–44 Midday.

1–10 A puzzle.

2–3 A boy's name.

4–5 A compress.

6–7 Name of a Southern State.

8–9 An exclamation.

13–14 To permit.

22–18 Look back upon.

24–25 Assessed upon.

31–32 A term of address.

41–34 A pronoun.

11–12 To invade suddenly.

15–16 To bring together.

20–21 A guard.

29–30 Pointed.

35–36 A Spanish epic.
38–39 Preposition.
46–47 What we see through.
48–49 An explosion.
50–51 Able.
52–53 Possessed.
54–55 The sum given.
56–57 A discussion of terms.
58–43 A nickname.
45–59 A Japanese island.
60–61 A canvas shelter.
62–63 To boast.
64–65 A waiting place for passengers.
22–23 An Arabian physician.
33–34 A way out.
13–32 To declare.
26–25 Cover.
 8–78 A beverage.
17–18 In what way?
 4–14 To boil slowly.

 2–9 A newspaper paragraph.
 3–11 An armadillo.
 5–15 Jacob's brother.
19–20 Writing fluid.
12–28 To expire.
27–29 A drink.
16–35 A poem.
37–38 To send out.
21–40 A town in France.
56–60 Aptly.
54–70 To blow upon.
66–67 To give a command.
42–43 Sad.
72–73 To bark.
74–75 Past tense of eat.
76–77 A preposition.
44–45 Days gone by.
68–69 A Goliath.
57–61 Past tense of get.
55–71 Conclusion.

as obscure abbreviations. This thorny issue came to a head when a desperate constructor came up with "GPJU" as an entry; this acronym stood for the Grand Potentate of the Johnstown Union—not exactly a catch phrase even among erudite solvers. Offenses of this sort had to be stopped, or the pleasure of the game would be diminished. Then there was the use of foreign words; unless they were familiarly used in English it was decreed that they be kept to a minimum. All definitions had to be taken directly from the dictionary so that solvers could check their work easily.

After World War I, *The World's* format changed, and with it the location of the cross-word puzzle. (While the crossword itself became a fixture at the newspaper, its spelling vacillated between the hyphenated "cross word" and the three-word "cross word puzzle" well into the 1930's.) A more comprehensive Sunday magazine subsumed the "Fun" supplement; crossword and mathematical puzzles were relegated to the "Ingenuities" page. During 1917, 1918 and 1919, crosswords consisted of separate miniature puzzles consolidated by a superimposed dark frame. No real interlock existed between the islands of words; the black squares served merely to connect these self-contained blocks (Fig. 14).

A curt editorial note on May 23, 1920 indicated that recent crossword puzzles had fallen into a rut: "Our puzzle fans are getting on such familiar terms with the dictionary that the puzzle maker has to resort to strategy." This tacit plea for more challenging entries spurred readers. A July puzzle included the names of four Presidents; in August, a puzzle by Louis Naveja of Woodhaven, New York, featured several Spanish words and thereby expanded the usual crossword vocabulary. Teams of two or more joined in the effort to improve crossword quality; such collaborations were heartily approved by the management, who believed that to avoid errors construction should be a two-man job, with one looking up words and the other fitting them into the diagram.

But despite the growing reader response to the crossword puzzle, the *World* staff continued its policy of benign neglect. Typographical errors, omissions, mismatched clues and other unspeakable offenses continually brought floods of letters from irate solvers. At last, an exasperated Wynne decided to wash his hands of the whole mess; he had taken the brunt of blame for the puzzle for seven years and was more than weary of it. He was also probably irked by the criticisms that flubs drew from one of the puzzle's regular fans, New York *Tribune* columnist Franklin P. Adams (F.P.A.). Rarely did a discrepancy escape the eagle eye of F.P.A., who chose to publicize the mistake in his "Conning Tower" column. Anyway,

Wynne reasoned, if the puzzle was to be a permanent feature of *The World*, as it evidently was, it was about time someone made sense of the chaotic crossword department instead of letting it continue in its characteristically wayward manner.

As a replacement for himself, Wynne recruited his stepdaughter's former college roommate, Margaret Petherbridge, two years out of Smith. Since she was a novice, he presumed that she would have more time to devote to checking the crossword for oversights—and what better way to learn the trade? On his recommendation, John Cosgrave, editor of *The World*'s Sunday magazine, hired her as his secretary.

Directly after her graduation, Margaret Petherbridge had got a job with Guaranty Trust. After being instructed to file "Coty Frères" under "F," she decided that banking was not for her. A crash course in shorthand qualified her as a secretary; she hoped that her position with Cosgrave would be a stepping stone to breaking into journalism. And so in January of 1921, when she discovered among her duties an untidy drawerful of time-consuming diagrams and clues, she welcomed the opportunity to promote her career.

Knowing nothing of the crossword, Petherbridge selected Sunday puzzles for visual appeal rather than content. Since she never stopped to solve a puzzle herself, they continued to appear with clues missing or misnumbered. Although letters of complaint never ceased to fill her in-box, she remained unmoved, convinced that only cranks would take the time to write on such a subject. It was not until the caustic F.P.A. joined the *World* staff in 1922 that she began to have pangs of conscience. F.P.A. had always been quick to point out oversights, and she had simply ignored them. But once he moved into the office next to hers he never lost an opportunity to take her to task.

"When he discovered that I was responsible for the crosswords," she later wrote, "he formed the atrocious habit of stalking in every Monday morning bright and early (about eleven o'clock) to point out to me in sarcastic tones just what was wrong with yesterday's."

Finally, she tired of F.P.A.'s gibes and determined to put an end to the matter. She began by trying to work the puzzle selected for the following Sunday. Before long, she learned how frustrating it could be to encounter such maddening obstacles as omissions and typos. For several hours she pored diligently over the disorderly papers, attempting to solve the puzzle. Once she felt properly initiated, she resolved to put an end to the past regime of hit-or-miss. With her left hand on the dictionary, she vowed to

TOP

1–7 The windpipe.
8–9 To establish by law, to institute.
10–11 A liquor made of malt.
2–8 Abbreviation of "errors excepted."
3–10 Prefix meaning "again" or "anew."
4–12 Act of selling.
5–11 A high playing card.
6–9 Abbreviation of "New Testament."

BOTTOM

2–3 Used in a ball game.
4–5 A girl's name.
6–12 An old soldier.
4–7 A pronoun.

2–8 A wager.
1–9 A man.
3–10 A suffix meaning "three."
5–11 Abbreviation of "North America."

RIGHT

2–4 A light quick stroke with the hand.
5–6 A spice.
7–9 Small.
1–10 A young ox; to direct.
3–8 A unit in cards.
2–7 The foot of animals having claws.

LEFT

2–4 A public house.
5–6 To excite.

7–9 A high explosive.
1–10 Hilarity; fun.
3–8 A prefix meaning "not."
4–9 The egg of a small insect.

C E N T R E

3–4 Abbreviation meaning "that is."
5–6 Abbreviation of "company."
7–8 Abbreviation of "New York City."
9–10 Colonel.
11–12 A head dress; a membrane.
13–14 Dismal, terrible, dreadful.
15–16 To lay up; to pack.
17–18 To be fond of.
19–21 Black.
22–24 To sympathize.
25–27 Old ropes untwisted and pulled loose into fibres.
28–29 Still; in addition.
30–31 Title given to distinguished aviator.
32–34 Powdery substance to which a body is reduced by fire.
35–37 The opening between the threads of a net.
38–40 A string of cord used in fastening boots.
41–42 Not strong.
43–44 A fuel.

45–46 To endure.
47–48 To ensnare.
49–50 To permit.
51–52 Untruth.
53–54 Abbreviation of "olive-drab."
55–56 Abbreviation of "chartered accountant."
1–11 A metal.
4–15 A young hawk.
8–19 Clever.
12–20 A dolt, a lout.
16–25 To court, to make love to.
21–28 Denial; refusal.
26–33 A two-masted vessel.
30–37 A tree.
32–42 To request.
36–46 Organ of hearing.
35–50 Flesh of animals.
41–54 An undesirable plant.
45–57 A blemish.
2–14 To draw gently.
5–18 The inner part of a thing.
9–24 An incorporated town.
13–23 A speck; a small point.
17–27 Indistinct.
22–29 To place.
31–38 A fish.
34–43 A pouch.
39–47 A portable bedstead.
40–51 A nobleman.
44–55 Belonging to the laity or people.
48–58 The sound of a bell.

herself to edit the puzzles to perfection. Never again would a puzzle appear without first being tested on the page proof by its newly inspired editor. It was the beginning of a most illustrious editorship. All that Cosgrave had hoped for was someone to proofread the puzzles before they hit the stands; he hadn't bargained on someone who would make this typesetter's headache into an international pastime.

In keeping with its modest beginnings, the crossword continued to make inconspicuous progress. Petherbridge had no trouble attracting contributors from among the ranks of regular fans. Although she modestly denies credit for her role in the scheme of things ("It was Wynne's acorn that sprang that great oak," she has since observed), without her the crossword would have died of neglect. Many of the basic structural devices as we now know them emerged in those first years of the Petherbridge reign. The most significant improvement was the shift to the single number clue. Rather than the unwieldy "7–13" to indicate a seven-letter word, the number "7" alone would represent the clue. "Radical," an anonymous fan, suggested this alteration, which Petherbridge adopted in the summer of 1923. At the same time she introduced the use of overall interlocking letters. She led constructors away from building large puzzles out of smaller independent shapes and encouraged diagrams of a more cohesive nature. Black squares ceased to frame words and began to indicate their end instead. Experimentation showed that symmetrical patterns provided the best diagrams; soon they became the standard (Fig. 15).

Nineteen twenty-four marked the year that the crossword puzzle skyrocketed to nationwide eminence. Later, after the dust had settled, F. Scott Fitzgerald wrote: "By 1927 a widespread neurosis began to be evident, faintly signalled like a nervous beating of the feet, by the popularity of crossword puzzles." Unwittingly, Petherbridge took the puzzle to its next logical point of evolution by compiling an anthology.

This chain of events began when Richard Simon and Max Schuster, recent Columbia Journalism School graduates, embarked on a joint publishing venture. Ushering in the New Year of 1924 as business partners, they opened a publishing house. Except for a lone typist, there was nothing in their small West 57th Street office to distinguish it as a place of business. On the evening of January 2, Simon was invited to dine at his Aunt Wixie's, a meal that was to prove pivotal to the history of the crossword, if history is to rely on human memory.* Aunt Wixie appealed to her nephew for some professional advice: Where could she get a collection of cross-

*Mrs. Farrar is skeptical about the veracity of Simon's anecdote.

word puzzles? Her daughter had become an avid fan who lived for the weekly puzzle in *The World*, and Wixie thought that a collection would make an ideal gift. But she couldn't find such a book. Simon reflected that he had never seen a publication of this sort, but promised to make inquiries first thing in the morning.

The next day he discovered that there were no crossword-puzzle books, and approached his partner with the proposition that they venture into this uncharted terrain. First, they decided to consult the expert in the field, Margaret Petherbridge, and see if she would help them. Much to their surprise, she was amenable to such an undertaking. She and the two other puzzle editors at *The World*, Prosper Buranelli and F. Gregory Hartswick, agreed to collaborate on a collection for a grand advance of $25 each; constructors would receive the honor of a by-line. With three editors at the helm, the anthology would certainly be ready by springtime.

Petherbridge's coauthors were distinguished members of the newspaper staff. Prosper Buranelli, known as "Pros," was a rotund feature writer who specialized in music but also showed considerable skill at composing charades and devising clues for treasure hunts in Central Park. F. Gregory Hartswick, editor of the "Red Magic" cryptogram section of *The World*, constructed puzzles under the pseudonym "Gregorian" (Fig. 16), edited them and even wrote a novel about the crossword-puzzle contests that were to become so popular in the late twenties.

Once the publishers had secured this trio of editors, they set out to get the endorsement of a public figure, suggesting to F.P.A. that he write a short introduction to the book. Despite the passion he had often expressed for the game in his column, Adams refused. Convinced that the book would fail abysmally, he took Petherbridge aside and advised her to abandon the idea. Already hard at work to meet an April publication date, she thanked Adams for the tip but followed her own instinct to see the book through. Discouraged by Adams's response, Simon and Schuster were on the verge of abandoning the project when they thought to investigate his past track record. They discovered that he had also advised the New York *Evening Mail* against hiring Rube Goldberg. On that note, minus an introduction, they went ahead with the book.

Yet the partners were still uneasy, perturbed by the general skepticism of their experienced colleagues. To protect the integrity of their publishing house, they decided to issue the book under another logo. Should it fail, the Simon and Schuster reputation would remain unscathed, and they could easily bury the incident. Besides, they reasoned, they didn't want to

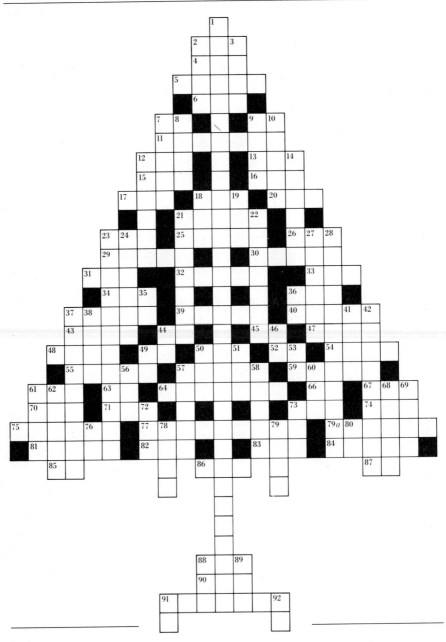

2. Def. article
4. A color
5. Shabby
6. Plaything
7. Part of "to be"
9. You
11. Large number
12. Obstruct
13. Small barrel
15. Employ
16. Australian bird
17. Beast of burden
18. Evil
20. Yea
21. Leaves
23. Starting point in golf
25. To decree
26. However
29. Glory
30. Malicious burning of a building
31. Burned coal
32. Tilted
33. Swab
34. Part of the foot
36. Sign of the zodiac
37. Wept
39. Occurrence
40. Quartz
43. Hits
44. In the year of Our Lord
45. Unit of measure
47. English college
48. A Roman emperor
49. Exclamation of surprise
50. Hotel
52. Part of "to be"

54. A sign of the future
55. Slight depressions
57. To assume
59. A diseased person
61. Observe
63. Iowa (abbr.)
64. Huge animal
66. Behold
67. Received
70. A vessel
71. Past
73. Pastry
74. A medieval shield
75. Writing implement
77. Disinfect
79a. Mean
81. Between 12 and 20
82. A fish
83. Part of the head
84. Melodies
85. Steamship (abbr.)
86. A cereal
87. Credit note (abbr.)
88. A lubricant
90. Sorrow
91. Small freshwater fishes

V E R T I C A L

1. Six-word title of especial interest to Sunday puzzlers
2. Jogging pace
3. Small whirlpool
7. Accumulate
8. Deep mud
9. Bond
10. Foe
12. A dry measure
14. Visitors

18. Prohibition
19. A month (abbr.)
21. Petalous
22. Written law
23. Tokens of respect
24. Repetitions of sound
27. Reverence
28. Formation of words by sounds
35. Editor (abbr.)
36. Rear Admiral (abbr.)
37. Beliefs
38. Scarce
41. A large book
42. Vigorous
44. Exclamation of delight
46. Mother
49. Like
50. A tavern
51. A fruit
53. Master of laws
56. A children's game
57. A disinfectant
58. Weird
60. Yale
61. Fat
62. Eagles
68. Brine
69. Large casks
72. Lyric poem
73. By
76. Within
78. Snake-like fishes
79. A buffoon
80. North River (abbr.)
88. To possess
89. A man's name
91. I
92. Therefore

F I G U R E 16 ▪ *Schuster Series No. 1, 1924 crossword by "Gregorian." A note to the puzzle states: "An all-over double interlock with a triply-locked center and corners. Probably considerably easier to solve than to construct. The words are weak in spots, but the construction passes the few obsoletes." © Simon and Schuster, 1924. Reprinted by permission of Simon and Schuster, a Division of Gulf and Western Corporation.*

H O R I Z O N T A L

1 Alternate passage
6 Incomplete
11 Fruity nut
12 Those who dry by wind
14 Cheerfulness
15 Capable
17 Midday
19 Man's name
21 Mountain in Greece
22 Passage-way
23 Negative
24 Shaped like a bull
27 Prefix, of
28 Character in *Peer Gynt*
30 Pits
31 Prefix, footed
32 Pert. to month
34 Settings
36 Plaything
37 Chemical compound
38 Imbecility
41 Sharpshooters
44 Annual Scottish festival
45 Adjusted
47 Consume
48 Ounce (abbr.)
49 Salts of stearic acid
51 Toward
52 Chinese tree
54 Hobo (slang)
55 Pert. to African people
57 Jog
58 Flat part of boat's bottom
60 Color

61 Taxes
63 Mistaken
65 Cook by air and heat
66 Awe-inspiring

VERTICAL

1 Oil
2 Fuse
3 Thus
4 Those in power
5 Naval officer
6 Decanters
7 Furrow
8 Abraham's birthplace
9 A form of colored cotton
10 God of Love
11 Form of sugar
13 Fuse
14 Ash kokos
16 Entrance
18 In want
20 Empower

22 Compounds of arsenic
25 Mineral
26 Dye
29 Finished
31 Active volcano of West Indies
33 Male descendant
35 Pinch
38 Dejected
39 Famous composer
40 Throw back
41 Knotty
42 Classification
43 Lay in a supply
46 European mountain range
49 Encounter
50 Brown pigment
53 Famous Scot
56 Outer coat
58 Egyptian god
59 To make a mistake
62 Exclamation
64 Concerning

make their name as game-book publishers. And so the book came out under the aegis of the Plaza Publishing Company (from the publishers' telephone exchange). Simon and Schuster had taken the gamble: now they had to build interest and amass orders.

Their scant budget made it impossible for them to hire a publisher's representative, so they solicited orders personally. Bookstores cautiously put in requests, reluctant to risk filling their stockrooms. One friend in a New York book outlet, in an extravagant and charitable moment, requested twenty-five copies. At $1.35 the collection came complete with a five-cent Venus pencil as a promotional gimmick; the pencil company had agreed to a contribution of 50,000 pencils on this basis. Also included was a penny postcard that could be mailed in for a set of answers. As the publication date approached, Simon and Schuster tallied orders: 800 copies in advance sales and a promise of 1,000 from the American News Company, a distributor. Not so great, but not as bad as they had anticipated, although they had a total of 3,600 books to get rid of. Free copies of the book were distributed at the American Booksellers Association convention in New York that winter, in the hope that orders would result.

In the heat of the moment, F.P.A. included a cheerful couplet in his April 10 column:

> Hooray! Hooray! Hooray! Hooray!
> *The Crossword Puzzle Book* is out today!

Except for one small ad placed strategically near the Sunday puzzle, there was no other advance publicity. The two publishers held their breath; in the event that their worst fears were realized, they were prepared to give the book a quick burial. Meanwhile, in honor of the occasion, they presented Aunt Wixie with a copy hot off the press.

Miraculously, the first printing sold out within the first twenty-four hours; in the next few months there were nine subsequent printings. The telephone never stopped ringing. New orders came from private citizens as well as booksellers. One year, three puzzle volumes and almost half a million copies later, the Simon and Schuster name proudly topped its Plaza pseudonym on the title page. (The Plaza logo was retained for sentimental reasons until Series #60.) On a single Christmas shopping day in December 1924 over 150,000 books were sold. In mock amazement, the publishers announced: "America is gasping for words."

Arthur Wynne was suddenly hailed as "father of the present craze." Stunned by his new-found celebrity status, he wrote a short piece on the subject. By the time the puzzle book appeared he had moved from *The World* to the Bell Syndicate, and so felt rather remote from the general stir. "I awakened recently to find myself acclaimed as the originator of the crossword puzzle. . . . All I did was to take an idea as old as language and modernize it by the introduction of the black squares," he modestly wrote. "I am glad to have had a hand in it, and no one is more surprised at its amazing popularity."

During this era of "Coolidge prosperity," America was rife with fads. "Yes, We Have No Bananas" was the hit tune; millions of Americans were chanting Émile Coué's optimistic slogan, "Every day in every way I am getting better and better"; President Coolidge was saying such uplifting things as "The business of America is business" and "When many people are out of work, unemployment results." The Teapot Dome scandal and Prohibition were the issues of the day; speakeasies drew an ever-growing crowd; mah-jongg, a recent import from the Orient, was the ruling game. Everyone who was anyone was getting out his set of tiles and calling up friends to come and play. How did the crossword puzzle manage to depose so established a craze? Mah-jongg manufacturers were baffled; they panicked as interest shifted and sales plummeted. Magazines kept their readers up-to-date on this dramatic turn of events, and taking advantage of this coverage, the mah-jongg dealers sent this lacy message to the crossword editors via the 1925 Valentine issue of *The New Yorker*:

> Roses are red
> Violets are blue
> We'd like to cut
> Your throats for you.

By the third printing, *The Crossword Puzzle Book* contained a "Warning" that alerted readers to the possible symptoms that might result once the contagion set in:

If you want to do any more work the rest of the day, put down this book now. If you insist on going ahead, say good-bye to everything else.

This is your problem: Do you wish to own a book which will delight and distract you, and perhaps shatter the serenity of your home, for at least one hundred hours?

"For a while there I was busy day and night constructing puzzles," Petherbridge is quoted as having said. For the next two years she continued to carry on her work both at *The World* and for Simon and Schuster. When she married publisher John Farrar in 1926, she resigned from the newspaper in order to devote her attention more fully to family life—as well as to the S & S Series, which was growing at a rate of two a year. The revolutionary effect of the series reached epidemic proportions; not only did the crossword puzzle books set Simon and Schuster firmly on its foundations, two other publishing houses—Farrar and Rinehart and later Farrar, Straus—were also launched on the profits. Wisely, Petherbridge handed over her initial $8,000 share to her father, a manufacturer of licorice powders and liquids, who invested the money in U.S. Steel and Standard Oil. Once she became Mrs. Farrar, her stockholdings were contributed to the establishment of Farrar and Rinehart. Much later, in 1946, royalties from her continuing crossword efforts went toward buying stock in the firm now known as Farrar, Straus and Giroux.

The World responded to the new demand for puzzles by instituting a daily puzzle on November 24, 1924. Gelett Burgess (of "Purple Cow" fame) was the constructor of the first one. To introduce it, he created an appropriate piece of doggerel:

> The fans they chew their pencils,
> The fans they beat their wives,
> They look up words for extinct birds—
> They lead such puzzling lives.

Commenting on the new daily feature, F.P.A. remarked that if it didn't put an end to unemployment, the editors would be hard-pressed to find a replacement. On this note, other newspapers succumbed to the rage.

Many people were beginning to shake their fists at the distracting puzzle. One football coach blamed it for sabotaging practice. On Broadway, chorus girls were missing cues for the same reason. The magazine *The Living Age* discussed the general havoc as viewed by Pottleby, who represented the legendary curmudgeon. Businessmen were puzzling instead of working, he complained; wives were careful to shut themselves in all day, the better to concentrate on the clues. "Statistics of the future . . . will undoubtedly afford evidence to prove more homes have been broken up, more folks driven to drink, more crimes committed, through the introduction of the crossword puzzle into our daily lives than through any of the catastrophes which punctuate the poignant pages of The Martyrdom of Man," he warned.

On September 27, 1924 a group met to establish The Amateur Cross Word Puzzle League of America. Although the names of those present have been lost and the League disbanded after the initial meeting, the group did leave a list of rules that have been applied ever since:

Rules for the Construction of Cross Word Puzzles

1. The pattern shall interlock all over.
2. Only approximately ⅙ of the squares shall be black (later modified to ⅙ or less).
3. Only approximately ⅒ of the letters shall be unkeyed (rescinded in the 1940's when such letters were outlawed altogether).
4. The design shall be symmetrical.

No facet of life was safe from crossword fever. In Pittsburgh, the Reverend George McElveen coaxed people to join his Baptist congregation by presenting his sermon in the form of a crossword on a large blackboard beside the pulpit. The oversize puzzle would be set up prior to the service for those parishioners who were interested in trying their hand at solving it and thereby enjoying a preview of the topic of the day. In Chicago, a judge sentenced the husband of "crossword widow" Mary Zaba to no more than three daily. Mrs. Zaba charged that her husband had been neglecting his financial duties and was suing for severance; Mr. Zaba denied the charge, but was forced to comply with the ruling of the court.

Fashion was not to be left out of this pervasive passion. Checked fabrics for dresses were in great demand, and crossword prints were not far behind. In New York City, one wholesaler featured a book of puzzles as a bonus to match a new line of crossword-decorated dresses. If the book was satisfactorily completed within a specified number of days, the shopper became eligible for a discount on future purchases. The perfect accessory for such an outfit was the attractive new crossword-puzzle jewelry described as "the talk of Fifth Avenue" (Fig. 17). Sterling silver collar pins were available for a mere fifty cents; more extravagant fans could sport fourteen-karat solid gold bracelets at a cost of $35.

The Elsie Janis Broadway revue, *Puzzles of 1925*, included a skit set in a sanitorium for crossword fans seeking a cure. This imagined scene may not have been as far-fetched as it appears—even the courts were disrupted by the contagion. One New York magistrate was faced with the frustrating task of distracting an intent group of twenty-one solvers in traffic court on a bleak January morning in 1925. When one defendant pleaded innocent to the charge that he had missed a prior hearing by explaining that he had had a longstanding engagement with a crossword, the judge promptly sentenced him to ten days in the workhouse.

FIGURE 17 ▪ *An advertisement for cross word puzzle jewelry, from the Simon and Schuster puzzle book, series 1. Reprinted by permission of Simon and Schuster, a Division of Gulf and Western Corporation.*

Another public incident was reported in a New York restaurant. One of the diners had brought the Simon and Schuster collection to the table for company; before long, two fellow solvers flanked him. The trio then blithely worked their way through the puzzles, oblivious to the din and the eventual sounds of closing time. Deaf to the pleas of the restaurant owner, they could not be persuaded to budge. The police finally managed to capture their attention by arresting the original offender. When faced with a ten-day jail sentence, the guilty party expressed delight at the prospect of uninterrupted solitary solving.

Journalists, baffled by the unprecedented attraction of the crossword, flooded the magazines with articles examining the quirky nature of the beast. What could account for the enormous appeal of this invention commonly praised as "the greatest known foe of boredom"? Ping-Pong and crokinole, better known as skittles, had long since come and gone without disturbing the status quo. *Literary Digest,* the distinguished weekly, assigned a reporter to investigate the case. By 1925, there were at least ten million fans in America, and yet there was no logical explanation for the fad. Even schools were beginning to succumb. The University of Kentucky voted to include crosswords in its curriculum; a Princeton professor had offered a prize to any student who could write a puzzle that would result in two legitimate answers to every clue. Dean Lough of New York University interpreted the overwhelming popularity as a modern expression of the human instinct for combat. "So the puzzle craze has swept across the U.S. like a devastating fire, consuming all in its path. What are the reasons that justify its existence?" asked the despairing reporter.

Psychologists at Columbia University came up with a theory that the crossword was a type of intelligence test; only those with a certain level of aptitude could participate. They used a group of unsuspecting students as guinea pigs. A crossword puzzle was distributed, and the students were instructed to fill in as much as they could until the stop signal was given. After thirty minutes, the papers were collected. The same group was then given an I.Q. test, and results were compared. The professors were happy to announce that those who scored best on the I.Q. test also rated high in crossword solving.

As for the impetus underlying a fad of this magnitude, the professors suggested that the clue seemed to lie in the word "prestige." Everyone wanted to be in on the latest thing. Already magazines of the day featured cartoons poking fun at old-fashioned mah-jongg players. The academic panel concluded with a brief overview: "The Chinese game first became popular on Fifth Avenue; bobbed hair came from Irene Castle and the movies; golf was the game of millionaires . . . And so it is not surprising to find that crossword puzzles received their first impetus from a well-known group of writers in New York. Though the puzzle had appeared more or less regularly in Sunday papers for over a decade, it was not until the writers picked it up that its popularity picked up." Indeed, by the early twenties, the names Robert Benchley, Emily Post, Gelett Burgess, Franklin P. Adams, Heywood Broun and Kathleen Norris figured prominently among the ranks of crossword fans. Once people of this caliber had linked their names to the game, it was not long before "smart" writing made mention of it as well, thereby making it a respectable pastime.

But it was the unceasing appetite for puzzles that really stupefied the world of journalism. A *Colliers* magazine article marveled at the breadth of the contagion: "A great war came and a great war went, peace treaties were signed and scuttled, statesmen arose and collapsed, new planets were discovered and lost, an eclipse arrived and passed—but the crossword progeny increased and multiplied and took possession of the land." Other experts viewed the crossword as an orderly oasis in a chaotic world, providing the same predictability as the math problem to the mathematician. All were agreed that the wave of accomplishment that flooded the solver upon successful completion of the diagram accounted for its irresistible attraction.

A vocal minority insisted on the vocabulary benefits derived from the game. With so much attention focused on the dictionary, how could it be otherwise? The average solver's knowledge was broadened, particularly in regard to the names of exotic animals. The motley crew of crossword pets included creatures of the most remote variety and even an occasional species. The director of the New York Zoological Society, William T. Hornaday, took it upon himself to compile a short descriptive list of the beasts; of the enduring emu he wrote: "The emu is to puzzle makers an ever present help in time of trouble. In the zoos he is even more popular." From ai to yak, these formerly obscure names were all familiar to the crossword contingent who soon committed them to memory.

The flurry of speculation about the crossword craze finally persuaded the crossword celebrities themselves, Petherbridge and collaborator Buranelli, to jot down their version of how it all began. Why had the crossword shuffled along for years and then suddenly, in 1924, begun to appear in dozens of America's newspapers? What accounted for the best-selling book? The rags-to-riches story was documented in the January 31, 1925 issue of *Colliers*. To start with, "the crossword addict is a savage correspondent." Concerned readers were responsible for the measures taken to upgrade crossword quality. To avoid irate letters, the editors were now careful to check for typos, incorrect definitions and omissions. Each diagram was systematically worked out on a proof sheet by the editor prior to publication.

When the same demanding solvers complained that most of the puzzles were beginning to look like isolated blocks of words inlaid into a superimposed dark frame, the editors were forced to take action again. Letters had to connect in one large cohesive grid to enhance the challenge of the game. Interlock was the key here, and "keying" the letters so that they worked in both vertical and horizontal capacities was the solution; otherwise the unkeyed letters (those surrounded by black squares) would dominate the diagram. Once the crossword was standardized to meet these basic qualifications, the quality improved markedly; and it was at this point that the puzzle was ready for mass consumption and distribution, as illustrated by the reaction to "The Crossword Puzzle Book."

Among the deeper reasons for such popularity the editors pinpointed a combination of recurring elements culled from their vast correspondence: a fascination with words, the desire for self-education and a penchant for killing time. Upon looking back at their experience in the field, they recalled the endless mail, mostly denigrating their valiant efforts. One critic even wrote: "The editors who allowed 'nearly' to be defined as a conjunction are—six-letter word beginning with 'r' and ending with 'n' and meaning terrible." (In other words, "rotten.")

Arthur Maurice, former editor of *The Bookman* (later replaced by John Farrar), hypothesized that the crossword had actually brought back to life forty words that had fallen between the cracks as a result of negligent vocabulary habits. He considered the resurrection of dormant words the most important factor in the evolution of the game. Before the crossword, it was the rare learned individual who knew that a cathedral contained an *apse* and a *nave*. Among those terms that were recycled he named *abet, ire, née, emit, err, elate*—words that have since been featured in thousands of puzzles. Not one was commonly used before crosswords helped put them back in circulation.

There was, however, a drawback to this type of overexposure. Soon many of these terms began to be reclassified as clichés. The crossword cliché became the bane of solvers everywhere. Oddly, although these words were recognized early on, they still irritate the solver and serve as the constructor's standby; the very composition of the words makes them invaluable in composing despite their bad reputation among solvers.

After the collection became a bestseller, F.P.A. created a dialogue that he felt aptly represented the omnipresent crossword cliché:

*Vocabulary Enrichment in the Suburbs Due to
the Crossword Puzzle Influence*

Mrs. Wordsworth: What is that you are working at, my dear?

Mrs. Frazee: I'm *tatting* Joe's initials on his *moreen* vest. Are you making that *ebon* garment for yourself?

Mrs. W.: *Yea.* Henry says I look rather *naif* in black.

Mrs. F.: Well, perhaps, but it's a bit too *anile* for me. Give me something in indigo or, say, *ecru*.

Mrs. W.: This torrid weather is very trying. One's vitality reaches its *nadir* in this heat, and to add to the discomfort I have an incompetent *serf* to contend with.

Mrs. F.: Oh, this *esne* problem. The last one I had was such a *schelm* I had to let her go. Would you drink a nice cold beaker of *negus*? I'm so *sere*. (And so on.)

Even *The New York Times* issued a brief editorial on this standardized vocabulary in early 1925: "There is only one river in this new cosmos. It is the Po . . . Egypt made her place in history secure by developing a bird named ibis and a goddess named Isis . . . There is only one world language worth speaking of. It is Erse . . . From the violence of the fever we gather that the crisis is near. Any day now it may witness a sudden subsidence in the passion and the tumult—we mean the vim and din."

Pouncing on the opportunity to promote their cause, The National Puzzlers' League rallied forces. Naturally, the new impostor did not have the ancient mystique of such traditional games as the word square and the acrostic. To prove their point further, members John Q. Boyer, Rufus Strohm and George Pryor compiled a handbook entitled *Real Puzzles* to counter the crossword craze. The runaway success of the crossword seemed to indicate a hitherto untapped public appetite for intellectual stimulation and entertainment; this book was designed to satisfy such a desire.

Without a doubt, 1924 was a year to be added to the calendar of American puzzledom, they announced; the previous years of importance included 1876, 1883 and 1920. The first date signified the original gathering of puzzlers on July 5, 1876 in Philadelphia; the second marked the establishment of the Eastern Puzzlers' League; the third, the year that the organization went national; and now this new wave of interest. Always a few years ahead of the national trend, the league's 1920 increase in membership had indicated that a craze on the level of the crossword was on the horizon. Nevertheless, the authors of *Real Puzzles* sought to reveal the obvious shortcomings of this elementary form of puzzle by exposing the monotony of its one-syllable words, its deviations into truncated or obsolete terms, its structural simplicity. The crossword was merely the first step in the enormous field of word-game construction, and at that it was only "a small unimportant section of Great Art." If only crossword constructors would use reference books instead of relying on a "limited vocabulary," their work would show greater variety, exhorted these old-time constructors; certainly, the crossword puzzle, when well crafted, possesses the same undeniable educational value as its exalted ancestors. If the crossword were to continue in its current style, these experts predicted that it would become "a stagnant pool covered with a floating scum of vocables with which the eye of the solver is already sickeningly familiar." Unless this handicap were to be resolved, doom would soon overcome the weak little game.

Hoping to attract the cream of the solving hordes, the new book offered 150 "real puzzles" of the old-school variety. To encourage participation, the introduction stressed that neither a college degree nor the experience of age had any bearing on becoming a puzzler of the first water; the acquisition of a good dictionary, gazetteer and a biographical dictionary saw to that.

But despite this genuine and valiant effort to divert some of the crossword energy to the pursuit of more "worthy" puzzles, the public was not to be distracted. The suggestion to consult reference books had already been taken to heart; many libraries were facing the perplexing problem of regulating the rush on dictionaries. Dictionary and thesaurus sales predictably soared, especially during the era of straight dictionary definitions (Fig. 18). For the avid commuter, an abridged dictionary was available as a type of bracelet. The main line of the Baltimore and Ohio Railroad installed dictionaries in each car of its commuter trains for the convenience of its passengers. Stocking up on crossword books before embarking on a long journey replaced the former custom of traveling with a few Victorian novels as companions. "Everyone is going about with knobs of knowledge sticking out on their foreheads like the buffers on a railway engine," observed one relatively objective witness.

Viewing the havoc safely from across the Atlantic, the London *Times* lamented that: "All America has succumbed to the crossword puzzle." In an article aptly entitled "An Enslaved America," it was reported that the crossword was a menace to Western civilization since "it is making devastating inroads on the working hours of every rank of society." When their New York correspondent estimated that, collectively, Americans devoted five million hours a day (most of them on office time) to poring over the puzzle, the British threw up their hands in horror at this threat to the industrial ethic. Trying to put an age on the dangerous creature, they concluded that the crossword must be some perverse result of the Civil War.

But even as they smugly dismissed the whole issue, the crossword insidiously invaded their shores via the pages of *The Sunday Express*. Arthur

Wynne had sold six puzzles to its syndicate, and except for a few alterations in spelling, they appeared intact. In this way, Wynne earned the title of original crossword constructor on both sides of the Atlantic.

By early 1925 the London *Times* was forced to eat its words: "The account was hardly printed before the craze had crossed the Atlantic with the speed of a meteorological depression." (Years later, the editors made a complete about face: "Who would have thought . . . that the crossword puzzle had come to stay? To most of us then it looked like a Transatlantic craze which could not be expected to take root in solid unimaginative British minds.") In an article in the New York *Evening World* Neal O'Hara declared that the crossword was only in its infancy and that before long daily papers would contain nothing but "gnus." And so in its inimitably modest way, the crossword invaded the international scene, leaving a trail of possessed solvers in its wake.

THREE

The British Crossword Puzzle

Upon returning to London after a brief stay in the United States in late 1924, a friend of journalist Robert Lynd reported in *The Living Age* on the strange goings-on he had witnessed; these observations first appeared in *The New Statesman*. A visit to anyone beneath the rank of President was certain to begin with a handshake followed by an unprovoked question such as: "By the way, can you tell me the name of a mythical bird in three letters ending in 'j'?" This curious behavior was precipitated by the new fad: the crossword puzzle. And a few months later, English newspapers began to import "what looks like a picture of a new kind of draughts-board or the signboard at the Chequers Inn, with mysterious numbers written in some of the white spaces."

Up until this time the acrostic had remained the predominant British word game; its prolonged reign was comparable to that of one of its greatest proponents, Queen Victoria. In 1923, acrostics were still providing material for an editorial in the London *Times*. "The 'shop' of Acrostics is today becoming a form of conversation in which all can join," remarked the editors. "More often than not [solvers] are left protesting that the composer has cheated them by some low device, some meaning of a word perhaps only to be found in an American dictionary." The predisposition was apparent: there was a regular contingent of puzzle solvers all over Great Britain in the pursuit of more challenging pastimes. The adoption of the crossword puzzle was inevitable. And, unlike its ancestors, it was made immediately accessible by means of modern communications.

One year after the acrostics editorial appeared, the crossword had deposed all other puzzles and usurped newspaper space. Its popularity was compared to that of jig-saw puzzles and detective stories. One observer even equated it with the Hampton Court maze, which also offered false starts. In London, crosswords enjoyed an unexpected vote of approval— from pickpockets. While engrossed in the clues, many dedicated solvers forgot to protect themselves from these sly experts. Pickpockets frequenting hotel lobbies in search of their prey even used a puzzle as a decoy to disguise their intentions.

Crosswords attained respectability when Queen Mary gave them a stamp of approval on January 13, 1925. *Time* magazine quoted from a press conference held by her Prime Minister, Stanley Baldwin: "I as Prime Minister and you as journalists are engaged in the common work of trying to elevate the people of this country, and you are doing it today through that marvelous medium, the crossword puzzle."

Before long the president of the British Optical Association, a Mr. Barker, alerted his colleagues to a new type of headache due to eyestrain and commonly associated with compulsive crossword-solving. The combination of the small type and the constant shifting of the eyes between clues and diagrams resulted in this unpleasant affliction. Mr. Barker concluded that the only possible treatment was moderation in crossword consumption.

As in America, dictionaries gained a new popularity, and libraries had to take precautionary measures against vandalism. One man marveled at the extensive search through various encyclopedias on which his nieces led him in pursuit of answers. In his opinion, the strain of researching was bound to drive the next generation mad. Even Noel Coward admitted that when he could make 1 Across fit with 1 Down, his day was made.

Among the crossword's many virtues, one of the most highly praised was its ability to enliven such otherwise crusty institutions as the Stock Exchange; it also provided a conversational topic between solvers seeking company. One ambitious fan decided to compose an address in good crossword-puzzle form; unfortunately, the postmaster did not accept the challenge and the letter was returned with a "no known address" stamp. "Already, without one's realizing it, the virus was spreading through one's veins," observed the London *Spectator* early in 1925.

American newspapers reported the spread of the crossword epidemic abroad. Budapest was the site of the most sensational incident. A temperamental young Hungarian waiter took his life, leaving behind only a crossword puzzle with a note indicating that the answers would provide the reasons for his action as well as the names of all concerned parties. The results of the puzzle (or whether it was ever solved) were not reported.

French newspapers warned their citizens to keep away from the dread crossword puzzle. In Vienna, the crossword was introduced by way of the coffeehouse. Customarily these establishments offer racks of browsing materials in all languages for the reading pleasure of their clientele. Many Viennese waiters had been interned in England during World War I and were therefore fluent in English. When the crossword first appeared as a regular feature, they were among the first to fall prey to its charms—much to the chagrin of impatient restaurant customers. Ireland organized a crossword contest in Gaelic, but despite the £5,000 first prize, no one was able to complete the puzzle, presumably because of the dearth of Gaelic dictionaries.

While these countries were delighting in the new game, the Italians were still blissfully enjoying the pleasures of mah-jongg. Their innocence of the crossword may explain the arrest of an Englishman going on holiday in Italy as late as 1930. He had carefully clipped out several newspaper crosswords for his evening's entertainment. The border official scrutinized one half-finished puzzle and decided that the man was an international spy. On this evidence, he refused the ardent solver admittance to his country.

Despite Queen Mary's enthusiasm, British editors still doubted that the fad would last out the year into 1926. By that time, they assumed, the ingenious Americans would have to come up with something else equally clever and fascinating. What they did not realize was that the crossword was evolving into a new form in the hands of a fellow countryman. Edward Powys Mather, a literary critic and translator, came upon the crossword puzzle as soon as it arrived in England and immediately recognized the host of possibilities intrinsic to that little diagram. It seemed to him that the most serious drawback in the puzzle of this period was the unimaginative definitions, which were simply taken directly from the dictionary. Mather recognized the latent potential for the exercise of wit here; he took it upon himself to experiment and examine these options, drawing on a lifetime of linguistic study. By mixing his great store of knowledge with a substantial dose of humor, he came up with a unique blend of ingredients in his definitions.

Straightforward clues were strictly taboo; puns and anagrams became the standard. One of his early clues for the word "saged" read: "The artist has been about cooked with herbs." The phrase "been about" indicated that the answer, read backwards, would give the name of an artist—in this case, Degas. The second half of the clue indicated the literal meaning of the word "saged." Other clues were written in verse, in the style Mather had developed in his days at Trinity College, when he had aspired to become an author. The combination of chronically bad health and the need for an income had deterred him from pursuing this career; now the creation of these ingenious clues gave him the opportunity to exercise his literary talents.

His first crossword efforts were circulated only among a small circle of friends. Among these privileged recipients was a literary agent, who suggested that Mather go public. At first he was reluctant—after all, he had a reputation to preserve as an academic—but he finally relented. Several of his fiendishly challenging puzzles appeared in *The Saturday Westminster*, over the signature "Torquemada" (the Spanish grand inquisitor). His first contribution met with a success that prompted the request for more, and the paper printed a total of a dozen "Crosswords for Supermen."

Shortly afterward, the *Observer* commissioned a few puzzles. By March of 1926 Torquemada was comfortably ensconced on the *Observer* staff, busily creating his famous series. He called his first few *Observer* puzzles "Feelers" to indicate the they were experimental and would be tailored to popular taste. Countless readers wrote to complain of the hours devoted to these impenetrable puzzles, while a small band of expert solvers begged for even harder ones.

The demand for an ever more difficult crossword irritated and challenged Torquemada. (Perhaps it was at this juncture that he decided that the crossword contingent was divided into highbrow and lowbrow groups.) Finally he decided to have his revenge by giving the highbrows what they were asking for. After some research, he came up with a puzzle that abandoned the elementary black-and-white pattern entirely; words were separated by heavy dark lines instead (Fig. 19). Since he had decided to discard the notion of symmetry in his diagrams, he felt that this new "bar" system looked better. He also dismissed the notion of letters keyed into two words. The key to the puzzle was wordplay and the humor it engendered; each clue had to be dealt with individually, since very few answers shared overlapping letters. In this way, Torquemada established the ground rules and the tone for the notorious British or cryptic crossword puzzle. The narrative style of crossword (also known as the bar diagram) became Torquemada's trademark, one which even his own disciples found it difficult to emulate.

F I G U R E 19 ▪ *No. 337, an example of "Torquemada's" fiendish constructions.*
It appeared in the Observer *during his reign there in the 1930's. Reprinted by permission*
of the Observer.

A C R O S S

1. They *are* wrung, hence the hesitation.
7. Each is smaller than a thief.
11. Was's royal rhyme.
13. 23.
14. Twelve of me go to a queen, yet twenty-four of my relations went to a king in one of me.

15.⎫
17.⎭ 7 ac.'s home.

16. Unchecked by the Bosporus and in 1 ac. and 1 dn.
18. Juggling with a trust that appeals to Scotsmen.
19. rev. Exchange of vulgar beast to wit when last is first.
21. The Oval seems the goal of my ambition.
22. A Scot counts his own ingredients.
24. Will nacht rhyme with.
25. Curve curved with 10.
26. Eventually part goes here and part to 30.
28. What I am is appropriate wear when I'm being used finally.
30. See 26.

32. Unchecked in 7 ac. and 28 ac.

36.⎫
33.⎭ Without issue and arrowy.

38. rev. Has wrote poetically in common with below.
40. Has wrote poetically in common with above.
41. See next.
42. Above featured with short Galsworthy play.

D O W N

1. You can make money by pounding this slush.
2. Name associated with next.
3. Lamb would do anything but die for me.
4. rev. Sir Philip Sidney's most loved and hated adjective.
5. rev. This feed comes to a correct conclusion.
6. Can be both objects of Pagan worship.
7. What the heroine of one of Shakespeare's plays was to that of another.

8. rev. The theatrical part that gives this word is often heavy.
9. How a horse can feel certainty.
10. See 25 ac.
12. One of no great shakes.
14. rev. 19 rev. or turn over.
20. This firm sounds as if it could ride.
23. 13.
25.⎫ I have a part in most of
34.⎭ Noel Coward's plays.
27. The grit in de Musset's machinery?

28. Months from hope.
29. rev. This Indian province wandered further when it wasn't good.
31. If you dot me one, I become Torquemada's favourite fare.
35. Arrangement of 13.
37.⎫ A halmaturus playing half
39.⎭ is seldom this.
38. rev. Timeless finish of my ac. rev. and 40.

If his followers found his handiwork enigmatic, they were even more curious about the creative process. Everyone wanted to know how he set (British for constructing crosswords) these monstrous puzzles, what the secret formula could be. But Torquemada remained tight-lipped until the end of his life. Years after her husband's death, Mrs. Mather revealed the well-guarded information. The procedure took place mainly in the master's bedroom. Each puzzle took about two hours to construct, although Torquemada preferred to work only about an hour at a sitting. Despite his enormous output, he never hired an assistant; his only collaborator was his wife. The master would select a topic and then compile a list of pertinent words. Mrs. Mather would scan the list for the words she liked, and once she had weeded out a sufficient number, she would construct a suitable diagram. Torquemada would sit up in bed, "looking very like a somewhat relaxed Buddha," and study the puzzle in question. When a word came to mind, he would add it to a handy list. Another of his favorite working places was the garden, in which he would sit "drawing marginal decorations in vari-colored chalks while he [brooded] on some uninspiring word."

Of the thousands of clues used over the years, only a small fraction were written by readers who submitted "revenge" puzzles. Skimming through the *Observer* series, Mrs. Mather discovered a word that had appeared fifty times without one repeated clue! Often the clues contained a theme that enhanced the end-product; they were never simply a group of unrelated terms.

The escalated challenge of Torquemada's work did not deter legions of determined solvers from tackling his new invention. Weekly, the *Observer* offices were flooded with thousands of completed diagrams vying for the first three winning positions that were awarded prizes. These numbers did not even include the estimated 2,000 readers who shunned the competitive aspect of solving. Answers arrived from as far away as West Africa, India, Alaska—wherever the *Observer* might be found. Torquemada published a total of 670 puzzles in the *Observer* during his lifetime.

It was, of course, only a matter of time before the contagion spread to that bastion of dignity, the London *Times*. Not given to adopting "trendy" causes, the editors were growing edgy; the crossword had outlasted all predictions and was showing signs of becoming a permanent cultural fixture. Editorial policy had to be carefully reexamined in this new light. On January 16, 1930 a letter to the editor appeared from a Lieutenant-Commander A. C. Powell. In it, Powell challenged the *Times*'s conservative attitude. Where was the weekly crossword? he wanted to know. His letter ended with the suggestion that they publish one daily.

For the next few days the editors tallied the letters received in response to Powell's request. Those in favor of a crossword puzzle led by four to one, and still more letters of support were pouring in. The debate continued to dominate the "Letters to the Editor" page with the pro faction in the lead. An occasional Scrooge would temper the enthusiasts: "Let me entreat you to keep the *Times* free from puzzles of all sorts," enjoined a Mr. Miller. "Space there is precious and prestige also." But by January 22 the editors were convinced that a crossword would be well received, and they announced it as a regular feature. In a bold marketing step, they even decided to include it on a daily basis, beginning on February 1, to counter competition by *The Daily Telegraph*. (Crosswords had appeared in the *Times Weekly Edition*—a supplement sent to the outposts of the Empire— as an experiment since January 2.)

After the *Times* had committed itself, the next step was to locate a qualified constructor. (Finding a crossword editor had been easily resolved by changing the responsibilities of the former aeronautics correspondent.)

In the search for a constructor, *Times* assistant editor Robert Barrington-Ward consulted Robert Bell of the *Observer*, where Bell had been composing the "Everyman Puzzle" to temper Torquemada's more abstruse entries. Bell appealed in turn to his twenty-eight-year-old son Adrian, possibly going on the assumption that the knack for constructing puzzles was hereditary. Adrian, then working as a farmer in the outlying area of Suffolk, and author of a novel entitled *Corduroy*, good-naturedly complied (Fig. 20). (In retrospect, he mused, "I had no idea then what an ideal occupation for dreaming up clues was harrowing ten acres of clods behind a horse that stumbles and nods.")

With a ten-day deadline and no previous experience young Bell came up with a standard cryptic and went on to produce thousands of puzzles through the decades that followed. During the early years he had to submit two puzzles a week, being paid at the rate of three guineas each. Later his assignment was increased to four, with other constructors filling in the rest of the week.

To prove that their standards were by no means deteriorating, the *Times* at first requested puzzles in both Greek and Latin. Presumably these esoteric crosswords did not attract the average solver, for they were soon replaced. Since the daily puzzle was published without a by-line the identity of the constructor became a popular topic of speculation among fans.

F I G U R E 20 ▪ *The London* Times *No. 1, published in February 1930. It was constructed by Adrian Bell.* © *The London* Times, *1930. Reprinted by kind permission of* Times Newspapers Ltd.

A C R O S S

1. Spread unevenly.
4. Part of a Milton title.
10. A month, nothing more, in Ireland.
11. He won't settle down.
13. 22 down should be this.
15. Cotton onto, so to speak.
17. Head of a chapter.
18. Denizen of the ultimate ditch.
21. Frequently under observation.
23. What's in this stands out.
25. Flighty word.
26. If the end of this gets in the way the whole may result.
27. Retunes (anag.)
30. This means study.
33. Simply enormous.
36. There's a lot in this voice.
38. This elephant has lost his head.
39. A turn for the worse.
41. Done with a coarse file.
43. Red loam (anag.)
45. This rodent's going back.
47. Makes a plaything with its past.
48. Wants confidence.
50. A mixed welcome means getting the bird.
51. This girl seems to be eating backwards.
52. The men in the moon.
53. A pinch of sand will make it dry.

D O W N

2. Heraldic gold between mother and me.
3. Out of countenance.
4. Upset this value and get a sharp reproof.

5. Intently watched.
6. In some hands the things become trumpets.
7. A religious service.
8. This horseman has dropped an h.
9. Sounds like a curious song.
12. This ought to be square.
14. Momentary stoppage.
16. Written briefly.
18. Calverley's picturesque scholars carved their names on every one.
19. Site of 45 across.
20. Precedes advantage.
22. Parents in a negative way.
24. Used to be somewhere in France.

28. Happen afterwards.
29. Climbing instinct in man.
31. A terrestrial glider.
32. The final crack.
33. The little devil's on our money.
34. Simplest creature.
35. Time measurements.
36. Jollier than 4 across.
37. Ladies in promising mood.
38. Presents are commonly this.
40. Gets the boot.
42. Hail in Scotland may mean tears.
44. Works, but usually plays.
46. She's dead.
49. Only a contortionist could do this on a chair.

Among the scores of letters sent to the *Times* on this matter was one from solvers Norman and Edith Campbell who patched together this portrait by analyzing the clues: "He is a man between fifty-five and sixty, educated at Eton and Oxford. In his youth he read for the Bar, but does not practise the law. . . . We have sometimes suspected that he is the secretary of an organisation connected with the stage. He has no young children. . . . He may even be a bachelor, for his interest in women seems to be confined to their hair."

Adrian Bell's identity was a well-guarded secret until 1970, when the *Times* at last decided to run an interview with him. In it, he recalled how his father had greeted his fiancée with the remark, "You have the sort of mind which will help Adrian with his crosswords." In fact, Mrs. Bell proved to be an apt assistant in her husband's crossword efforts, and although Bell modestly attributed the prestige and wit that came to be associated with the *Times* crossword to its editor from 1930 to 1960, Ronald Carton (who was succeeded by *his* wife, Jane), he did observe later that a wife, "if she has the mind to, can make herself almost essential to a setter."

Throughout his career, Bell's greatest professional expense was one dictionary a year; they invariably fell apart after twelve months of steady use. In retrospect, Bell assessed his career with the observation, "I think you must be near dotty to spend your life setting crosswords" (Fig. 21).

According to one *Times* reader, the general crossword following is an "eclectic, versatile, whimsical, cultivated fellowship—an audience of intellectual magpies," involved in a never-ending, albeit good-natured, struggle with the constructor "in which the last thing that anyone wants is a final victory for either side."

The debut of the early Wynne-style puzzles in 1925 spurred immediate competition among avid British solvers, who succumbed to the charms of the crossword. The director of the Bank of England, Sir Josiah Stamp, claimed to have mastered the early puzzles in *The Sunday Express* within fifty minutes—with some help from his family. Nobel Peace Prize winner Sir Austen Chamberlain clocked himself at forty-one minutes. This craze later caught on among *Times* crossword-solvers. Most impressive was the claim of Montague James, a former provost of Eton, who allegedly completed a *Times* crossword while his four-minute breakfast egg boiled. "While the school may have been Eton," quipped another solver, "I am quite sure the egg wasn't." In response to this remarkable feat, P. G. Wodehouse complained: "To a man who has been beating his head against the wall for twenty minutes over a simple anagram, it is gall and worm-wood to read a statement like that one."

While *Times* readers showed off their skills, other crossword minds were busy at work devising new stumpers. In the vanguard of this movement was the BBC publication *The Listener*, vehicle for the legendary "Afrit," Alistair Ferguson Ritchie, headmaster and prebendary of Wells Cathedral, who has been hailed as the originator of the modern cryptic clue. A noted scholar with a well-stocked mind, Afrit's abilities equaled those of Torquemada (Fig. 22).

Not much is known about Afrit except that he died before he had the opportunity to put his crossword theories on paper. He did, however, publish one book, *Armchair Crosswords*, in which he outlined some of his innovative ideas. Most famous of these is his dictum, derived from Lewis Carroll's Mad Hatter, that "You need not mean what you say, but you must say what you mean," which is indeed the essence of the cryptic clue: although the clue may seem deceptive, it must read coherently to "say" what it "means." The words can—and do—appear different from their intended meaning until the clue is successfully deciphered, at which point the entire answer should fall neatly into place. Unlike their forerunners, these clues are no longer simple definitions but clever ruses that require some mental gymnastics. W. H. Auden once remarked that although cryptic clues are more complicated than their American counterpart, they are more precise. Auden was absolutely correct: there are no extraneous words in cryptic clues. While they may appear convoluted, once resolved they make perfect sense. The straightforward term "solvent," for example, has been disguised as "Able to pass with credit in Latin and French; an effect of sun and wind."

Afrit's motto engendered the so-called "square dealer" philosophy that currently prevails among British puzzle-solvers. This unwritten code stipulates that no matter how obtuse or tricky the clue may be, the answer must be recognizable to the solver as an idiom, cliché or other familiar term; originality is invested in the clues rather than the answers. A mundane answer such as "electricity bill" would be spruced up by the fanciful clue "Charge of the light brigade." (In America, the trend has leaned to the opposite pole; aesthetic diagrams and tricky answers have taken precedence over clues.)

When Torquemada died in 1939, a trio of experts inherited his throne. Within six years, one of these master craftsmen had usurped the entire domain. Derrick Somerset Macnutt, Senior Classics Master at Christ's

FIGURE 21 ▪ *The London* Times *"Golden Jubilee" crossword puzzle, 1980, commemorating fifty years of puzzles in the* Times, *was also constructed by Adrian Bell.* © *The London* Times, *1980. Reprinted by kind permission of Times Newspapers Ltd.*

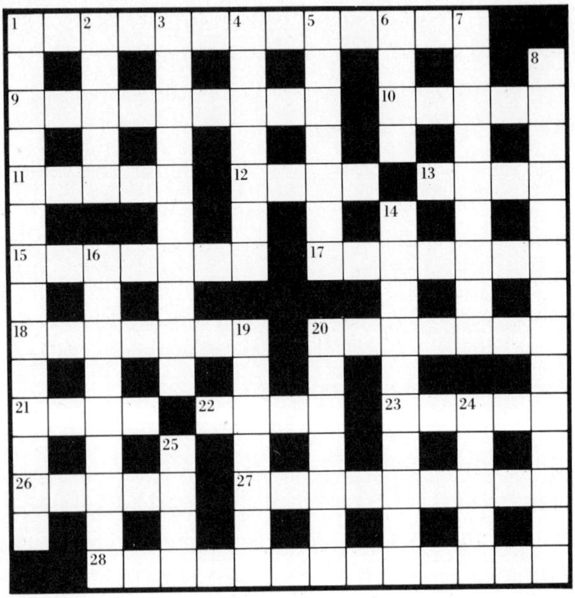

A C R O S S

1 Never a cross word in 1887 (6, 7)

9 Lay of Midas's ocarina? Or of one of 1 down (6, 3)

10 A once gold coin I love in Latin American locality (5)

11 Alloy as might be attached to a sovereign (5)

12 Inscribed 'I promise to pay' back—for its school fees? (4)

13 Gustave the golden (4)

15 To wit his written work gives us the splits (7)

17 A glistering performer on the breakers is not necessarily golden (7)

18 Nut of the jeunesse dorée (7)

20 Maybe a 9 to attract more, if one doesn't cut the cackle (4, 3)

21 Not the Golden Rose, but a different sort, love (4)

22 The this, said Hamlet, is a golden quality (4)

23 A Thomas (trigger-happy?) in odd company (5)

26 Character of wood, hoof and horn (5)

27 The Golden Treasury, by Burlington House musicians (9)

28 Straitway into heaven for US, St Francis? (3, 6, 4)

D O W N

1 Lots of silly females, though one could make a valuable deposition (7, 2, 5)

2 £3, nothing in that and short of yen, for suckers (5)

3 Synonymously gilt-edged perhaps, to be a sight better off (10)
4 They express no golden opinions (7)
5 Poe's gold one gone missing among the flora? (7)
6 If gold is it likely to fall? (4)
7 Eruptive isle of exile of 20-franc gold piece, so to speak at length (9)
8 E.g. Britain on the gold standard? (9,5)

14 Shelled wreck of a sun-car, etc. (10)
16 Apparatus of golden reflections (9)
19 Not 'my bow of burning gold' in 'Jerusalem', just the quiver (7)
20 Unfestive cake, it's observed (7)
24 Looking-glass messenger from Manhattan (5)
25 A lustrous prize to tempt Selima (4)

FIGURE 22 ▪ *"Armchair II" by "Afrit."* The Listener's puzzle No. 866. A note appearing with the puzzle states that *"No dictionary should be needed, and the solver is required to complete the diagram. The stops are blacked-out squares arranged in a four-way pattern which looks the same whichever side of the diagram is uppermost. Two-letter spaces are not clued."* Reprinted from Ximenes on the Art of the Crossword Puzzle *by D. S. Macnutt, by permission of Methuen & Co. Ltd.*

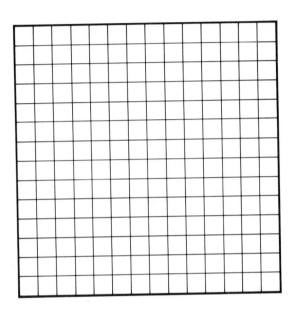

ACROSS

1. Often its cure is affected by things which are not what they seem.
8. Five "heroic stanzas" take a hundred in once: I am taking a hundred in twice.
10. Your ration of meat, perhaps: a couple of pounds in the popular stores.
11. Able to pass with credit in Latin and French: an effect of sun and wind.
12. Its wealth is fantasy, old age or trouble its realisation.
13. First catch your deserter, then give a shout of triumph: thus you show your sense of proportion.
14. As Tweedledee would have it, you'll find Somerset a-losing matches to a certain extent with places apart.
17. The liner captain may say you can eat off his; if so, you must have cake, mind!
20. Mr Smith of ancient Rome; Mr Publisher of modern London.
22. Describes the liner captain in actual fact, but not in actual order.
24. Give a tanning to—not M. Jones, nor M. Robinson.
25. Just a song at sunrise. If you know it you won't say, "Oh, good!"
26. Was the Maid of made of fats . . . ?

27. Marrowfat monarch but the other way round between two points, permitting communication between two points.

D O W N

2. Something to eat for a maisonnette in 'Appy 'Ampstead.
3. A cat's life is supposed to be, so the River's not clearly in sight, not even if old.
4. Very mysterious, of Little by Little with somewhat turned-up toes.
5. Don't get fed up about a small account: adverse circumstances have to be.
6. Follow Shakespeare and give to reverse of airy something—well, a local habitation and a name.

7. Have a look round the pool before you put a foot in.
8. It runs trippingly half way and the rest is done in the head: that should be in solving it.
9. They make a ring round Mother and ring traps son!
15. You keep quiet about the family one, but after you have let on there's no more to be done.
16. Pretty little tune about the beef extract which prevents that sinking feeling.
18. They're disturbing, alas, when you don't see the funny part.
19. Chemical which gives an idea of the speed of insect reproduction.
21. In the matter of this tree a graduate has nothing on Sir W.S. Gilbert.
23. Not a great head of water, but there's an extra head of smoke.

Hospital School, proved himself worthy of the position. He had already anticipated the possibility of this momentous takeover by adopting the *nom de plume* "Ximenes," the name of the original Torquemada's successor in the Spanish Inquisition.

Ximenes had a long and fruitful career. At a salary that ranged from ten to fifteen guineas a puzzle, he made fortnightly contributions to the *Sunday Observer*. Each opus took him about one-and-a-half hours to construct. Clues extended from pure cipher to anagram to outrageous pun; much of Ximenes' reputation was based on his well-publicized sense of humor. For example, his clue for "Onega": "I'm wet but I'm only half ga-ga!"

Although Ximenes had learned his craft from Torquemada, he adhered to Afrit's style where clues were concerned. In his definitive book, *Ximenes on the Art of the Crossword Puzzle*, he admits that he began by remaining absolutely faithful to Torquemada's *modus operandi*. He admired his mentor greatly; he never ceased to feel that the completion of a Torquemada puzzle was a legitimate cause for pride. But after using Torquemada's system for a while, he concluded that "one must be oneself," and from that moment on instituted some of his own policies. He credits Afrit for his change in attitude (although he allowed that Afrit's puzzles were beyond his ken as a solver for the most part). Torquemada had relied heavily on intuition as a guide to crossword construction, while Ximenes realized that he worked better with a set of rules. He tactfully remarked that "rules of cluemanship are [relegated to] ordinary mortals, and not the likes of the great Torquemada."

In his early days, Ximenes felt that he "erred" by using clues that were too obtuse or obscure and therefore not fair to the solver. But the course of the British crossword shifted after one of his fans, L. E. Eyres, personally introduced him to Afrit, an event of which there is unfortunately no account. This gesture so touched Ximenes that he dedicated his book to Eyres (Fig. 23).

According to the British crossword Bible, *Chambers Twentieth Century Dictionary* (or *Chambers Crossword Aid* for the more avid fan), a clue is a "thread that guides one through a labyrinth." If the answer is completely unfamiliar to the average solver, then the "thread" is useless. After studying Torquemada's clues, Ximenes divided them into three categories: (1) the verbally agile (precursor to the modern style); (2) the literary (most often Torquemada's favorite authors); (3) the straightforward definition (which Torquemada occasionally used when he was at a loss for a more sophisticated one). This last type was often the most tricky, for readers were on guard for deception and often misinterpreted such straightforward tactics. As a result, the clue "Will nacht rhyme with" could easily mislead the solver away from the answer, "yacht." On the other hand, a clue of the first category could require quite a bit of legwork. "What I am is appropriate wear when I'm finally being used (5)." (The number of letters in the answer is indicated after each clue as a convenience to solvers.) The answer here is "black suit"; in five letters, it becomes "spade." Clues in the second category often entailed some knowledge of Shakespeare, as in this example: "Wore a russet mantle in Shakespeare (4)." The correct answer, "morn," refers to Horatio's speech in *Hamlet*, in which he says, "But, look, the morn, in russet mantle clad,/ Walks o'er the dew of yon high eastern hill." (*Hamlet*, I:1).

With both Afrit's and Torquemada's theories to draw upon, Ximenes soon incorporated the two styles into his own. While he agreed with the former's policy on clues, he enjoyed the variety offered by the latter. He also objected to the length of Afrit's clues. "A good short one beats a good long one every time," he declared. (Later he confessed that this preference might have been artificially acquired during the World War II paper shortage.) He further experimented by using unkeyed letters (those surrounded only by black squares) in the style of Afrit for at least part of the diagram. Each clue then had to be worked out individually to make up for otherwise overlapping letters. To be fair, only single letters were treated in this way and not two or three in sequence, so as to add some challenge without diminishing the fun of solving. Ximenes also reinstated the use of symmetrical diagrams, scorned by Torquemada, in which he continued to use clues of the first type.

Ximenes instituted an award on a regular basis to be presented to the reader who could replace a straightforward clue with a cryptic one. The record number of entries was 900 and the minimum never dipped below 200. The first prize (a book token worth about $3.50) was presented to the solver who submitted a successfully completed diagram along with an original clue. Ximenes' personal favorite contest entry was a vertical one sent in by a Mr. E. Gomersall which defined "madcap" as "Cake with nuts on top." Expert Will Shortz speculates that this inscrutable clue can be explained with the use of *Chambers Dictionary*. According to Chambers, "cake" can mean "fool," a direct reference to madcap; in a vertical position, with "nuts on top" yielding "mad," the answer emerges again.

Ximenes, like Torquemada, was sensitive to his audience, which he

ORIGINAL CLUES

ACROSS

1. Dash, said the bully, I've missed my target! [5].
5. City of romance in which one of the Camerons was laid low [7].
11. Such a black and blue excrescence is common to idlers of all ages[10].
12. Set on an attempt to make money [4].
14. Thin drink [6].
15. Rob a stringed instrument of its compass-points with poor results [6] . . .
16. . . . and put them round a spinner to get the best out of a vein [5].
17. Fishy answer to a nautical poser? [8].
19. Just look at Henry! Wasn't it beastly! [6].
20. Butter-dish offered to doomed captain was (pre-rationing) [6].
22. The sort of affection you don't want to have at your fingertips [6].
25. Shakespearean captain, with a scar on his left cheek, will make us untrue [6].
27. Refraction of the spectrum, reacting well to heat [8].
29. Much attached to Gladstone [5].
31. Holds the fort, retreating to capture a knight [6].
32. "Gowns, not arms, repelled/the fierce —— ——" from Rome [6].
33. You need more than this single old buckle-catch for lifting [4].
34. (2 words) Its members don't like a money-keeper to become verbal; see also 18 [10].
35. Formerly parliamentary on Wednesdays [7].
36. I can make this wrong crockery prophetic [5].

DOWN

1. People made long journeys to see that of a prospective daughter-in-law [7].

2. Changed Sedley into Osborne into Dobbin [6].
3. Affix in two parts a scrap in one [5].
4. Is the ability to succeed as flighty as it sounds? [8].
5. Inclined to be tenacious, as absorbed by Jones after work with Mrs. J.'s permission? [6].
6. Open-mouthed at the bill [6].
7. It looks comparatively stupid to make oneself so hard to follow [6].
8. Important city of Czecho-Slovakia [4].
9. What we call those who issue from crashed planes [10].
10. Plane crash at a great height [5].
13. They plot, so that we may know what it's been like and what to expect [10].
18. What made the wood so, giving it 30 or 34? Slope did, of course! [8].
21. Not spent, ywis, in seemless amenance by its user! [7].
23. Punish for violating Lent in France [6].
24. Pertaining to a vital disturbance [6].
25. Aimed to mislead the electorate [6].
26. How to deal with an unsatisfactory conservative set in the kitchen! [6].

27. Uncle Peter's former name [5].
28. The way to end a letter from Mexico [5].
30. See 18 [4].

REVISED CLUES

A C R O S S

1. Heavy blow, but the bully misses his target [5].
5. *Romance Capricieuse* for violin, *not* krummhorn [7].
11. Once crooked, slippery customer—results of borrowing produce . . . *what* sort of hump in idlers? [10].
12. Set on an attempt to make money [4].
14. Once round the tiles for a drink [6].
15. Mean companion—a trial [6].
16. Extract step by step what's precious in enigmatic poets [5].
17. Fishy answer to a nautical poser? [8].
19. Look at Harry—it was horrid [6].
20. Old miniature railway renovated in lavish style [6].
22. Nasty skinny portion, one ounce, sent back [6].
25. Captain isn't false without us. All's well—capital [6].
27. Breaking up the spectrum, they react well to heat [8].

29. Strip is out of date: a slip's the thing nowadays [5].
31. I hold the fort, retreating to capture a knight [6].
32. Pyrrhus, for example, in one direction advanced from east to west [6].
33. Chinese secret society's gripping leg [4].
34. (2 words) It includes naval men, brisk, with a roll [10].
35. Being an old retired man, about a hundred [7].
36. Excavation in Greek site—if only I were there [5].

D O W N

1. People came miles to see Katisha's horse in it [7].
2. A professional footballer, name of Booth [6].
3. Affix in two parts a scrap in one [5].
4. Sounds flighty, but shows the ability to succeed [8].
5. Being tenacious, I'm always in pocket [6].
6. Like a bill when opened, after someone's cooked it—the account—right and left [6].
7. To speak with a first suggestion of menace [6].

Clues to Figure 23 continue on page 82. **8 1**

8. Important city of
   Czecho-Slovakia [4].
9. *Spring* love inflamed
   one? The opposite—
   kind of ice [10].
10. Plane crash at a great
    height [5].
13. Rods round love-curve
    may indicate a storm
    [10].
18. What made it what it
    is? Slope did, perhaps
    [8].
21. Might give Tony hug,
    showing former
    freshness [7].
23. Fine gossamer cell's
    endoderm [6].
24. Eastern European girl's
    had her tail pinched
    [6].
25. Tried—hush!—to
    practise piracy [6].
26. Be up in anger—the
    best way to deal with
    an unsatisfactory
    conservative set [6].
27. Conservative outcast?
    Cut short: name
    disused [5].
28. This tough part of a
    letter may be omitted
    [5].
30. Sage must be cut
    slantwise [4].

likewise divided between those who enjoyed the crossword puzzle simply as a diversion and the more passionate devotees—a division that he felt applied to the acrostics fans of the past as well. Whereas the former group was content to work out clues when there wasn't a good book around, the latter placed the puzzle above all other preoccupations and relished the use of reference books and texts. Ximenes geared most of his work toward those serious followers whom he later cultivated as friends and correspondents through the *Observer* contest. For the less avid solver, he created the "Everyman" series—puzzles designed to be worked out "on a park bench, in bed, on a train journey"—in other words, without access to dictionaries.

Another Ximenes innovation was the annual dinner given in honor of his steady following. This event provided his fan club with equal time to debate the clues and answers that had appeared throughout the year. *Time* magazine covered the occasion of his 200th puzzle, which was celebrated in September 1952 at the Café Royal in London. Sixty fans milled about, ranging in age from twenty to seventy, from clergymen to bank clerks, all united by a common passion for Ximenes' puzzles.

Ximenes himself was easily recognizable by a badge marked "Mr. X" and his rimless spectacles. He opened the proceedings by begging for forgiveness for a certain 26 Down which read "Earnest money got by leaving deposits on old clothes." Complaints regarding this impenetrable phrase had poured into the *Observer*. Taking this opportunity to defend himself, Ximenes pointed out that "deposits on old clothes" referred to "dye"; "get money" is easily defined by "earn" which when taken from "earnest" leaves "-est." The logical outcome of this operation yields the answer: "dyest." Definitions that received applause included such clever ruses as "An important city in Czechoslovakia" which is correctly answered "Oslo," if the reader takes the hint literally.

Once they were pacified, the group absolved Ximenes and even went so far as to thank him for the outrageously difficult puzzles that dominated their Sundays. One fan exclaimed poignantly, "It's impossible to imagine what our lives would be without you." Despite all the kudos, Ximenes, like Adrian Bell, observed that only "a lunatic with a distorted mind" could devote his life to constructing the fiendish little puzzles.

Although Ximenes died in 1972, his dedicated followers continue to carry on the tradition of the annual dinner. The cryptic crossword puzzle has become such an integral part of routine life to the British that the dinner represents the gratitude of tens of thousands of fans.

Once the British public realized that the best way to relieve the monotony of recurrent answers in the crossword was to make the clues less transparent, the early American puzzles were left by the wayside. From the start, the London *Times* puzzle could be decoded only by first unraveling the anagrams and riddles in the clues. From this introduction, the British solver developed a deep suspicion toward words: double meanings lurked behind each one, no matter how insignificant it appeared. A simple entry such as "apex" may be disguised in the deceptive sentence, "It is topping to kiss a monkey." Reducing the hidden clues to their rudimentary forms, the answer emerges as "ape + x." In this case, the x represents the "kiss"; the first part of the clue provides the literal definition of "apex," thus reinforcing the answer.

Free association seems to be the key in conquering these inscrutable puzzles, and a strong literary background is a valuable asset. One early reader imagined the ideal team he felt could handle a puzzle during a nine-mile train commute: a general informant; an expert in modern literature, anagrams and farming terms; and a classicist. Indeed, skilled detective work is called for, combined with a shrewd sense of humor and, if possible, a familiarity with philology. Once the clue is resolved, the feeling of accomplishment may stay with the solver for years; favorite clues linger in the minds of puzzle devotees for life.

Not everyone is so fortunate as to master the British puzzle en route to work. One Fiji woman completed the London *Times* puzzle of April 4, 1932 in May 1966, after thirty-four years of hard work, according to the *Guinness Book of Records*. Former *New York Times* crossword editor Will Weng admits that he can't even get to first base with them. Sir Max Beerbohm expressed his frustration by constructing a revenge puzzle of mostly nonsensical terms. This nightmarish creation appeared in the London *Times* in 1940. Sir Max addressed a letter to the editor in which he suggested that the editor must sometimes be tempted to enforce—perhaps even abuse—his powers. "And you may have at some time thought: 'Suppose I released into the columns of *The Times* . . . a Crossword Puzzle with clues signifying nothing—nothing whatsoever,' and may have hideously pictured to yourself the effect on all the educated parts of Great Britain?" Beerbohm went on to paint a glum picture of listless men at the best London clubs, sitting in a stupor. The revenge would be heightened by the addition of some reasonable clues tempering the completely nonsensical ones. Such a monster might even affect the course of the war, he speculated. And so he undertook to create the beast himself. The editors decided to print the crossword, but to undermine the maliciousness of such a ruthless step, they printed Beerbohm's incriminating letter along with it (Fig. 24).

In 1947, the London *Times* moved the crossword from the middle of the paper to the back page, reportedly leading one delighted follower to exult: "It is no longer necessary to open the thing at all!"

At this point in its evolution, sociologists ceased to analyze the redeeming factors of the crossword puzzle. Solving was no longer considered suspect or a waste of time. On the contrary, it had established itself as a prestigious pastime. One addict proudly responded to an inquiry regarding educational credentials with "on the back pages of the *Times*."

From its debut in 1930, the London *Times* crossword has maintained a reputation as "the most famous puzzle in the world," and the basic British crossword puzzle has not changed significantly since. One reader sent in a request for a subheading to read: "Clues and answers should not be discussed in public," objecting to those vocal solvers who accidentally gave away answers while collaborating in public places.

Inspired guessing and hard work should bring success to the determined cryptic crossword-solver once the basic shorthand code is mastered. First of all, the reader must acknowledge that each clue consists of two parts: the direct and the indirect reference, with the latter presenting a play on words. These two options offer alternate routes to the answer. One part of the clue should be read literally for the direct reference; the other should be examined for wordplay.

Inherent cleverness overrules general knowledge; each clue presents a riddle, pun or double entendre—in other words, a miniature puzzle within a larger puzzle. Humorous double meanings are the heart and soul of the cryptic crossword. For example, the clue "Heavy shell out—dollar finished (8)" disguises the simple answer, "buckshot." Once this special sense of humor is acquired, clues become more accessible. For the constructor, the reward of a cryptic lies in writing a well-polished definition that makes literal sense while camouflaging an otherwise simple term. If it is any consolation to the frustrated solver, composing an ingenious clue is time-consuming: hours and hours are spent on the diabolical diagrams by the constructor before the puzzle ever reaches the solver.

A preliminary familiarity with key terms is required in order to enter the cryptic crossword arena well armed. Each of the main categories of clue is signified by a specified device that becomes clear as the solver's

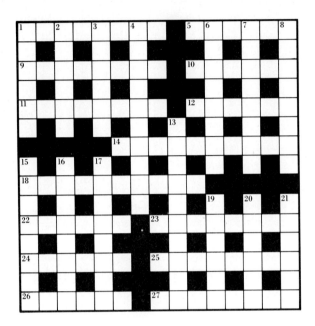

ACROSS

1. A Victorian statesman lurking in a side lair (8).
5. Milky way unseen by star-gazers (6).
9. An insect with a girl on each side (8).
10. Pugilists' wear (6).
11. Four toes are broken (8).
12. The cockney's goddess appears to have been a slimmer (6).
14. There's a little company in the meadow next month (10).
18. "But what if memory Itself our ——— —s had betrayed?" (Matthew Arnold) (two words) (5, 5).
22. A nudist's aunt? (6).
23. "That day he ——— the Nervii" (Shakespeare) (8).
24. Acknowledgement of debt in a vessel (6).
25. Neither animal nor mineral, and only three-fourths vegetable (8).
26. Not what the wicket-keeper tries for in Essex (6).
27. The P.R.A. is utterly confounded (8).

DOWN

1. Drum (Newbolt) (6).
2. The top of the morning, perhaps (6).
3. A Manx beverage (6).
4. Ho! Let's go in (anag.) (10).
6. Wordsworth's fan mail? (8).
7. And yet sugar *can* be refined (8).
8. They are up and doing, no doubt, in 'the sweet o' the year' (8).
13. Little Tommy thought it meant a red-faced blacksmith (10).

15. Voltaire's *prêtre enragé* (8).
16. Such buns are eaten on a good day (two words) (3, 5).
17. Caliban's sea-change (8).

19. Pollarded haven (6).
20. I'm in the old Roman bath (6).
21. "Our ——— clues that do but darken counsel" (Tennyson) (6).

The letter from Max Beerbohm which accompanied his spoof crossword ran:

"No doubt you, like most people, have sometimes thought of some utterly awful thing that you *could* do if you chose to, some disastrous and devastating thing the very thought of which has brought cold sweat to your brow? And you may have at some time thought: 'Suppose I released into the columns of *The Times*, one of these fine days, a Crossword Puzzle with clues signifying nothing—nothing whatsoever,' and may have hideously pictured to yourself the effect on all the educated parts of Great Britain? You may incidentally have seen yourself going into your club shortly before luncheon-time and observing in the armchairs men with blank, set, fixed, pale, just-not-despairing faces, poring over the current issue?—one of them perhaps rising unsteadily and lumbering out to the library and asking the librarian, 'Have we a Wordsworth concordance?'—or some question of that sort. You may have figured this man going home at tea-time and his wife saying, 'Oh, Stephen, is anything the matter?' He: 'No, dear, nothing.' She: 'But you look so pale. You—' He: 'I've had a rather hard day, dear. But I'm quite all right.' And you may furthermore have wondered just how the apology in next day's issue should be worded—just what excuse should be offered, before the shutters in Printing House Square were briskly and slammingly put up for ever? Perhaps I oughtn't to remind you of this nightmare of yours. Forgive me.

"P.S.—The nightmare wouldn't be loathsomely complete unless a few of the clues were quite genuine—*and very simple*, so as to put the solvers in good heart, and make them confident of success, and keep their shoulders to the wheel. I have provided six such clues with my usual forethought."

skills improve; these categories are derived from the traditional word games that preceded the crossword puzzle.

The first category is the second definition. Not all cryptic clues are designed to drive the solver mad. Occasionally, the constructor includes clues that contain a double synonym. Two terms in the definition therefore indicate the answer, as in "use a CB nickname." The answer ("handle") is both a synonym for "use" and "CB nickname." This is the simplest of the clue categories.

When the constructor feels mischievous, this type of clue may be spiced up with a pun; a question mark customarily alerts the reader to this course of action. Punctuation can be very revealing—or misleading—in that the two parts of the clue are not in any way indicated and so must be recognized by the expert eye. The question mark punctuating this sentence by Will Shortz makes it a likely candidate for a pun: "One way to break a habit of Thanksgiving leftovers?" The answer ("cold turkey") justifies that suspicion. Ximenes' favorite clue was "He went to Hell—several of them in fact"; the answer was "Dives."

The second category, anagrams, is the most easily unraveled, since all the letters are already provided within the clue itself. Anagrams account for about 15 to 20 percent of most clues, although Ximenes warned against their overuse. In his opinion the ideal proportion was three or four to every thirty-six clues. Originally anagrams were labeled as such by the term "anag." in parentheses following the clue. However, this method was soon discarded as too transparent. Nowadays, the solver acts as a sleuth, checking for telltale signals that indicate an anagram. These include both the literal (broken, torn, poor, twisted, bent, out of order, upset) and the figurative (drunk, at sea, rioting). Other words that signify the presence of an anagram include: altered, clumsy, crushed, crumpled, disguised, flawed, given a face-lift, in a bad way, mangled, mixed, rebuilt, repaired, smashed, troubled, unruly, went to pieces.

"Writer's block produces mad poem," a clue by Jack Luzzatto, cleverly disguises the answer "memo pad," The first half of the clue offers a literal albeit misleading hint, while the second half "produces" the answer when the anagram is unscrambled.

Another type of clue that contains all the letters in the answer is the "concealed" or "hidden word" variety. Here, however, the letters are all in correct order once the well-trained eye spots the run-on answer. As in the case of the anagram, there are indicators that warn the solver of the presence of this type of clue; and again, there are two parts to the clue: the literal and the "hidden." Each of the following terms shows that the answer is at hand: hidden in, inside, camouflaged, falls into, in.

Ximenes warns the constructor that the concealed-word clue can be "hopelessly obvious" if not done to perfection, although it is a boon to constructors as the easiest way to define a dull word. But to the expert solver it may be too easy. An example by Ximenes exhibits the best aspects of this type: "Where they wear saris in th*in dia*mante (5)." The indicator "in" leads the solver to the answer, "India."

The word "in" plays a large role in cryptic clues. Not only can it indicate a concealed-word clue, it may also signify a container clue. What differentiates the latter from the concealed word is that the letters are *not* in sequential order; all the letters are represented but not as they will ultimately read. The Will Shortz clue "City that suits Ron in toto" yields "Toronto." The name "Ron" is "contained" by the word "toto" to yield the answer; *in* is the crucial word here. Other possible signposts are: about, around, among, grasped by, interrupting, surrounding. All of these terms imply that the correct answer will be found by investigating the combinations at hand. Most prominent are the terms *in* and *about*, which can be interpreted as the splitting of a word to insert a fitting syllable or two.

A trickier container clue, also by Will Shortz, reads: "Instrument of change around the newsmagazine (9)." The absence of the term "in" may be temporarily misleading; "around" is the key word here. By wrapping "alter"—the element of change—around "time"—the news magazine—the instrument, "altimeter," will appear. The first part of the clue, "instrument of change," yields the same result.

The anagram and its descendants, the charade and the logogriph, illustrate the influence of Victorian word games on the cryptic crossword. The charade breaks a word into its basic elements. These shorter words are then disguised in the clue; when the components are strung together, the complete answer emerges. Of course the clue must also offer an alternate path to the answer: it cannot simply present the essential elements alone. The London *Sunday Times* clue "The embassy receives a sign from heaven: must be religious types! (12)" is a good example of a charade. "Embassy" yields the word "mission," while "sign from heaven" is "Aries": joined, the two form "missionaries" or "religious types."

If the constructor feels benevolent, there may be some indication that the word will be revealed by the connection of the various syllables. Of course, the hint is subtle: "added to," "receiving," "joined up," may provide the missing link. If none of these phrases is present, there is no way to tell whether the clue is a charade except by trial and error; acumen and experience will ultimately see the solver through.

The logogriph may show up in the cryptic puzzle as a deletion in the form of a beheadment or curtailment. This translates as the omission of a letter at the beginning or end of a word and does not exempt dropping a letter from the middle of a word. Expressions such as "lose one's head," "headless," "beheaded," "doesn't start," "doesn't begin," signal that a beheadment is near. Then the solver must guess the possible response in order to be able to carry out the surgery. The prefix "un-" also signifies this process.

When a letter is dropped from the middle of a word, it may be indicated by a verb such as "leave" or "omit." If the letter "I" is to be deleted, it would be most easily signified by the phrase "I will leave." One example of a beheadment is the clue: "Possess a topless dress." The answer ("own") is reached by working backwards from the word "gown," which answers for "dress," and removing the "g" thereby making it a "topless" dress. The verb "possess" reinforces the answer.

Sometimes the answer to a cryptic clue may read coherently, from left to right as well as right to left. In that case, it qualifies as a reversal, and the clue will contain definitions for both words. Constructors often feature these words as Down entries. Consequently, the clue may reveal the versatility of the answer by signals such as "up" or "rising." If the answer reads Across, the solver should look for a sign of reversal by watching for a phrase that suggests backward movement, meaning that it will work in that direction as well; "back" or "returned" would be an indication.

Sometimes a clue may incorporate two categories, mixing an anagram with a reversal. For example, if the letters "mi" were needed in the answer, the clue might begin with the phrase "I'm reversing."

One Ximenes reversal reads "Heater with electric valve reflex—one just out (9)." The answer, "debutante," reads backwards as "etna tubed." The reversal is subtly indicated by the term "reflex."

A modern addition to the clue variations is the homophone, which extends wordplay to include sound. The phonetic aspect of the answer is signified by terms indicating the act of hearing. Among the most common signals are "we hear," "one hears," "I hear," "reportedly," "they say," "so it's said," "it appears," "from the sound of it." The solver must really be on guard for this hard-to-crack clue. A word such as "Eton" might be represented by the verb *eaten; aroma* could be disguised in "a roamer."

This example by Will Shortz captures the essence of the type: "Sausage is not the best, they say (5)." The answer, "wurst," cleverly combines the sausage aspect of the clue with its homophone, *worst*.

In addition to the general clue types, there are the standard phrases whose values can be easily deduced once the cryptic code is mastered. Abbreviations rank highly in this area. The clue remains inscrutable until the code is cracked. Experienced solvers therefore acquire a healthy knowledge of common British abbreviations. Occasionally a hint will be dropped: words such as "small," "minor," "quickly," "little," "shortly," "briefly," may give away the secret.

These indicators are only provided, however, when the abbreviation is not commonly used as a cryptic shorthand trick. Otherwise the solver must recognize that the abbreviation is implicit in the text. An innocuous word like "direction" or "point" means that one of the letters on the compass (E, W, N, S) is needed; "degree" may mean that the letters MA or BA are lacking. Other standard phrases to be aware of include:

```
zero, goose egg, love = 0
right = R
left = L
a, an, I = ONE
soft = P (musical symbol)
loud = F (musical symbol)
hundred = C
doctor = DR
Alabama = AL
little Diana = DI
tom = CAT
Royal Artillery = RA
Royal Engineers = RE
```

Hours of practice may be required before one is equipped to handle the cryptic. Until all—or the majority—of the possible variations and tricks become familiar, the solver must be prepared for a considerable time commitment. A special type of circuitous reasoning is necessary in order to conquer the cryptic. And yet the British are so accustomed to this type of thinking that the standard American puzzle seems as obtuse to them as the cryptic does to the American solver. But once the solver overcomes the initial hurdles, the fun begins. And when the block diagram like that offered by the London *Times* is conquered, there is always the bar diagram to contend with.

Some experts believe that the cryptic represents the wave of the future. In the hierarchy of puzzledom, the crossword pyramid rests on the broad base of the word-search and the easy crossword, building up to the more difficult *New York Times* Sunday puzzle and thereby to the cryptic crossword. The cryptic is not designed for mass consumption; it requires an elevated level of thinking that disqualifies it as popular fare. Because the extensive latitude offered by the clue structure makes it easier to recycle frequently used words, the cryptic is not handicapped by that bane of solvers, the crossword cliché. Should any of the standard fillers saddle an otherwise lively puzzle, the clue easily sidesteps the deadly effect of dictionary definitions. As newspaper columnist Neal O'Hara wrote in a 1925 piece, "No gnus is good gnus."

The adoption of cryptics in the United States began in 1960, when *The Nation* began to include them as a regular feature, allowing American cryptic fans to indulge themselves in this rarefied pastime. One such fan, Burt Shevelove, introduced fellow-puzzler and composer-lyricist Stephen Sondheim to the cryptic in this way. Sondheim became so enamoured of the idea that when, in 1967, Gloria Steinem asked him to construct a puzzle for the about-to-be-launched *New York* magazine he agreed—and promptly provided a cryptic, thus continuing to popularize the British-style crossword. When Sondheim could no longer spare the time from his musical duties, he ceded the position to Richard Maltby, Jr. Lyricists seem to have no trouble translating their talents to the cryptic crossword. Maltby, who wrote additional lyrics for the 1980 Broadway production of *Ain't Misbehavin'*, moved his crossword to *Harper's* in 1976. When his musical responsibilities prevented him from carrying the full load of crossword constructing, he joined forces with his editor, E. R. Galli, who had been test-solving the puzzles for about five years. The partnership was a great success, with Galli shouldering the construction of the puzzle while Maltby concentrated on the clues. Although Galli is certainly a proponent of the cryptic and has gone on to adapt an even more enigmatic type of British puzzle known as "RightAngle" (Fig. 25), he is doubtful that the cryptic will ever overpower its American counterpart. However, with such teams as Galli and Maltby at *Harper's* and the equally ingenious Cox and Rathvon at *Atlantic*, the cryptic is certainly gaining ground on American soil (Figs. 26 and 27).

New York magazine later adopted the London *Times* puzzle. While British solvers suffered without a puzzle during the 1978–79 strike,

R I G H T A N G L E S # 1 — T - S Q U A R E

The special twist of RightAngles is the way in which words are entered in the puzzle grid. Each word makes one right-angle turn somewhere along its length. But it's your task to determine where each word makes this turn and in which direction.

As a guide, the starting direction of each answer word (i.e., the direction of the word *before* the right-angle turn) is indicated by the letter given after the clue number. Words can go north, south, east or west to start with. Of additional help is the fact that each letter in the correctly completed grid appears in exactly *two* words, no more, no less.

For RightAngles #1, the actual words to be entered in the grid are listed and seven letters are given. But be careful—several of the words could cross those Ts in more than one way.

1W BLATHER	9S BASTOGNE
2W TABLET	9S BAIT
3S SAW TEETH	10E AORTA
4W TEA	11S RICH
5S WAPITI	12N HABITAT
6N PASTA	13N COOTIE
6W PAP	14S INGOT
7S REMADE	15W STITCH
8E BOTCH	16W DAME

FIGURE 26 ▪ *"Double Cross," a puzzle by Emily Cox and Henry Rathvon from* Atlantic, *August 1979. Copyright © 1979 by The Atlantic Monthly Company, Boston, Mass. Reprinted with permission.*

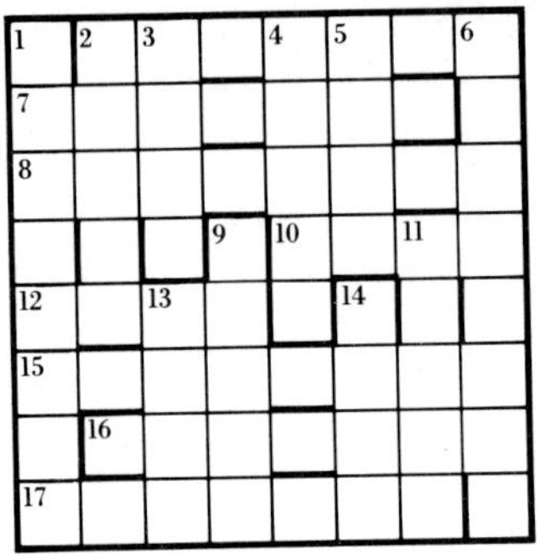

DOUBLE CROSS

Pairs of clue answers in this puzzle must share accommodations in the grid. Every square is occupied by two letters; in squares where answers intersect, each letter belongs to one Across entry and one Down entry. The solver must determine which horizontal answers intersect with which vertical answers. The order of each pair of clues is arbitrary, as is their order of entry in the diagram.

Answers include one common French word and one proper word. Punctuation may be used deceptively.

ACROSS

2a. You have choices about light in Double-crosses (7)

2b. Release granted from trap (7)

7a. Asked questions full of holes (7)

7b. Diamonds should follow otherwise, given that opening (7)

8a. A dressmaker's unhappy customer (8)

8b. Make indifferent boxer a teen Rocky (8)

10a. Double the circumference of the head (4)

10b. Cross pair of mules, e.g. (4)

12a. Someone singing flat, missing F, and moving on a whole note (4)

12b. A student's behind what's shown in nude sketch (4)

15a. Brood in . . . in . . . in sort of box (8)

15b. Being obsequious to one with one foot in the grave (8)

16a. Crooned melody in reverse, having some wine (7)

16b. With big nut, choke opening of elephants' trunks (7)

17a. Canada geese and unusual herons seen around central lakes (7)

17b. Retrace explosive supplier (7)

DOWN

1a. Cryptic acrostic pertaining to a certain Greek (8)

1b. Threateningly wave cereal bowl? (8)

2a. To get oddly amusing lift peer over lady's head (5)
2b. Greenish liquid containing bit of garbage in bottom of boat (5)

3a. Bet is taken up by two kings (4)
3b. Return of tendency to correct (4)

4a. Excessive amounts of food add pounds to stomachs (5)
4b. Wet plastic resin (5)

5a. Highest point is one around top of mountain (4)
5b. Aspiring writer keeps article in sort of tidy condition? (4)

6a. Generate riots in youth (8)
6b. He adores being furious? (8)

9a. Register with branch of a secret society (5)
9b. Scoundrel's defeat (5)

11a. Device for holding name inside clothes (5)
11b. In motion, one gets cooler (5)

13a. Barely sufficient, incomplete examination (4)
13b. Well-disciplined voice trained (4)

14a. Progress with diet (4)
14b. Raise voice with reproach for double-crosser, e.g. (4)

F I G U R E 27 ▪ *Another puzzle from the Emily Cox and Henry Rathvon "Atlantic Puzzler" section in* Atlantic, January *1980. Copyright © 1980 by The Atlantic Monthly Company, Boston, Mass. Reprinted with permission.*

R E S O L U T I O N S

Fourteen of the clues lead to answers that will not fit into the diagram until they have been resolved, in a way. These words include one proper noun. Other clue answers include two proper nouns. Punctuation may be used deceptively.

A C R O S S

1. Dark conger eels in a stony place (4, 6)
7. Skim a jazzy phrase (4)
11. In reforming Red China, Teng created a new order (12)
12. Daily coffee container has face on the outside (7)
13. Horse galloped around ring (4)
14. Fashionable party with a group that includes monarchs (7)
15. Naming members of the bird and fish classes respectively (7)
19. K-mart in Galesburg stocks riding gear (11)
20. Start artlessly, then complete speech with hesitations (7)
22. A cowpoke's home cooking is done here (5)
23. Butcher or banker: the unfortunate in love (11)
24. Readjust deck again (7)
26. Being permissive spoiled Al rotten (8)
30. Explain desperately, "It's all true" (10)
32. Fisherman's cord rises and rolls (7)
33. Use a bow tie (4)
34. About 42.8% of English old people can be employed (7)
35. Great monkey food (5)
36. Old woman sprints nimbly around end of race (8)
37. Fossil fuel found in sea bottom gushed up (6)

1. You should wash this kind of clothing and dry it off (5)
2. Change a latrine not tidied up (11)
3. With an instrument, try to catch fish (8)
4. Fancy suite with ornamental cases (5)
5. Emblem on jewelry is annoying (9)
6. Doctor covers American sailor with medicinal powder (7)
8. Apt 151 in rooming house located on Central Speedway (8)
9. Rest period precedes quick meal (9)
10. Leader of fallen angels in Pandemonium gets means of support (7)
16. Seattle's rank, swarming with vipers (12)
17. Red Alert ordered after onset of commandos (6)
18. Itch when wearing certain garments in lengthy measures (8)
20. Lester went out for a paper (10)
21. Most of the difficult part is finished (7)
24. Drapes arranged and filed (6)
25. Seek a phrase styled for a poet (11)
27. Disappear after sun dance (5)
28. Out West, bed mule in prairie plants (11)
29. The end of good quality (4)
31. In Jodphur, a lazy river (4)

American solvers blissfully worked puzzles retrieved from *Times* archives that predated the appearance of *New York*.

The intrigue presented by the cryptic lends it the air of a good detective story that few dedicated solvers can pass up. In fact, the cryptic puzzle has been considered suspect during wartime. One week before D-Day in 1944, British agents carefully examined the Sunday puzzle in *The Daily Telegraph*. For weeks solvers in the secret service had been aware of the appearance of several code names in that paper's puzzle. The code words for the Normandy beaches, UTAH and OMAHA, had both appeared. At the end of May, the code name for the entire operation (OVERLORD) was contained in the puzzle. And only seven days before the attack was to be launched, the 11 Across clue "This bush is a centre of nursery revolutions" yielded the word MULBERRY—the classified name for the two giant harbors that would be towed across the Channel.

The coincidence seemed uncanny. Two M.I. men decided to confront the traitor. They set out for the Surrey home of Leonard Sidney Dawe, who had been the main source of *Daily Telegraph* puzzles since the mid-1920's. Astonishingly, the whole issue was simply coincidence. After some discussion, the M.I. men went home satisfied that Dawe was innocent.

Although the cryptic crossword puzzle may project a cloak-and-dagger image, it is simply a tongue-in-cheek development of the basic crossword. From the start, British constructors were fascinated by the potential of the clue structure, whereas the American interest focused on the diagram. Once the aesthetic possibilities were exhausted, Americans turned to the clues with completely different results—and not without considerable experimentation.

Torquemada explained the differing approaches from the setter's point of view in an article that appeared shortly before his death in the February 1935 issue of *Fortnightly*. He divided the development of the crossword in England into three phases: (1) the initial craze; (2) the birth of the cryptic; (3) the growth and nurturing of the cryptic.

In Britain, after the first burst of interest faded among the general public, a small academic stronghold fanned the flames with more ingenious creations. The movement graduated to an accepted institution when "Mr. Punch" added a regular crossword to his magazine. "While the mentally edentulous still have their pabulum, the cerebrally dentiferous can now command a choice of daily bread," Torquemada declared. He ranked the crossword with "bad prose and good grills" as a reflection of the national character.

▪ F O U R ▪

Later American Developments

On January 4, 1925 the first Intercollegiate Cross Word Puzzle Tournament was held in the auditorium of the Hotel Roosevelt in New York City. With literally thousands of cheering fans in the audience, Yale beat Harvard, Princeton and The City College of New York. Harvard was represented by two distinguished alumni, the columnist Heywood Broun and dramatist Robert E. Sherwood, while poet Stephen Vincent Benét and Jack Thomas made up the Yale team.

The contest was held in rounds as each word was tackled individually. First Broun won a round by correctly guessing the name of a German poet in five letters (Heine); then Sherwood backed him up with a seven-letter word meaning "honest in intention" (sincere). A foul play was called when the judge, Ruth Hale (Mrs. Heywood Broun in private life), sat beside Broun. Toward the end of the ninth inning, each team had contributed to the completion of the puzzle with the exception of one word. The decisive entry was defined as "slight convex curve in the shaft of a column." In a moment of inspiration, the Yale team correctly answered "entasis." The crowd broke out in an old Eli hymn of victory as Broun called for a rematch.

Contests soon appeared in various newspapers as competitions for readership mounted. The first bold step in this direction was made by Bernarr Macfadden, publisher of twelve magazines including *True Story*, *True Romance* and *True Detective*. He also masterminded *The New York Evening Graphic*, once described by *Time* magazine as a "low-brow sheetlet." A man with an unerring feel for pulp, Macfadden cried "Meat!" upon recognizing the juicy potential of the crossword, and announced that *The*

Graphic would hold a crossword contest beginning in January 1925. This contest would be "the greatest ever," with $25,000 in cash prizes. For twenty-six consecutive days, a series of puzzles appeared in the paper. The first 2,619 people to submit a correctly filled-in series were the winners.

At the height of the contest, *The Bronx Home News*, a small, highly regarded tabloid, thought of a clever way to attract readers. Every day the staff would huddle over the *Graphic* puzzle until they had solved it. The next morning the completed crossword ran in their paper under the headline "Probable Answers." As a result of this campaign, the offices at *The Graphic* were deluged with piles of correct solutions. Macfadden suspected foul play and soon discovered the leak. His lawyers promptly appealed for an injunction to prevent *The Bronx Home News* from continuing to publish the contest answers. The appeal was denied. According to the judge, the puzzles were subject to copyright; the answers, which had never been previously published, were not. Neither paper was willing to give in: *The Graphic* continued to publish the puzzles, and the Bronx paper the solutions. Finally, the tension broke when *The Graphic* switched to a new puzzle contest in February, the object of which was to supply the last line of a given limerick. Apparently *The Bronx Home News* was not poetically inclined.

With the onset of the Depression in 1930, the promise of cash prizes for solving crosswords became increasingly enticing, and in late 1931 *The Chicago Herald and Examiner* recruited Eugene Sheffer to mastermind such a contest. Sheffer, who submitted his first puzzle to *The World* in 1924 when he was a sophomore at Columbia University, had become official constructor for King Features Syndicate three years earlier. At the time of the *Herald and Examiner* request, Sheffer was a professor at his alma mater and wondered how he would be able to manage the time off from his academic duties; fortunately, the assignment coincided with the Christmas break. *The Herald and Examiner* brought Professor Sheffer to Chicago on the "Twentieth-Century Limited" and set him up at a plush Chicago hotel, where he plugged away diligently for the next two weeks. Each day he produced part of a projected series of thirty crosswords based on a Declaration of Independence theme; each puzzle contained both the name of one of the signers and a key sentence from the document (see Figs. 28 and 29). At the end of the day, he made his way through the snow and wind to the newspaper office to hand in his work.

The first puzzle appeared on February 16, 1932, and a grand total of $5,000 in prizes was offered. The answers poured in, some of them accompanied by elaborate decorations; solvers were eager to distinguish their work for extra points. And these efforts were not overlooked: faced with thousands of correctly solved puzzles, Sheffer decided to use presentation as the decisive factor in the judging process. The success of the series prompted *The Herald and Examiner* to commission another such contest, and Sheffer found himself back at the construction board.

In the midst of all this activity, *Time* magazine reported the Silver Anniversary of the crossword puzzle, a term that in this case referred not to the number of years the puzzle had been in existence, but rather to the number of crossword books issued by Simon and Schuster. *Fortune* magazine published the story of how the unpredicted success of the series had set the budding publishers up in business. Series #25 appeared in 1932, and at this point, F.P.A. was glad to supply the preface that he had denied to the first volume. The crossword puzzle books had made history and become a publishing staple.

Editors Farrar, Buranelli and Hartswick had been busy compiling spin-offs ever since the 1924 best seller; *The Celebrities Cross Word Puzzle Book*, which appeared in 1925, made quite a splash, boasting puzzles set by such famous figures as Irving Berlin, Harry Houdini and Anna Pavlova* (Fig. 30). The following year the original "Three Musketeers" (as S & S fondly referred to them) dwindled to a pair, when Prosper Buranelli accepted a position with newscaster Lowell Thomas. The real energy behind the books, however, had always been generated by Margaret Farrar. Looking back, Albert Leventhal, the S & S games editor at that time, observed that the company had "needed a games editor like an Apollo spacecraft needs antimacassars," but Mrs. Farrar continued to live up to the high standards she set for herself. Concerned about his first meeting with the *grande dame* of crossword fame, Leventhal prepared himself for a headstrong personality, but within minutes of their first introduction she had won him over. Thereafter he took a back seat until he moved into the sales department, where he could be of real help to the crossword series.

Official acceptance of the term "crossword puzzle" came in 1934, when the entry first appeared in Webster's *New International Dictionary*:

cross′word (-wûrd′), *n*. A crossword puzzle.
cross′word puz′zle. A word-guessing puzzle, developed from the *word square* (which see), in which the words, when correctly supplied, cross each other vertically and horizontally, so that most letters appear in two words.

*Actually most of these puzzles were written by the three masters themselves, based on suggestions from the celebrities.

THE CHICAGO HERALD AND EXAMINER

OFFERS **$5,000** *in cash prizes*

and lots of fun for solving LIBERTY

CROSSWORD PUZZLES

Liberty Puzzles are easy, interesting, prof- itable! The name and picture of one of the signers of the Declaration of Indepen- dence, and a word from a key sentence in

that famous document, appear in each puz- zle. Just solve the puzzle and give the name of the signer and the word from the key sentence!

No. 15 Liberty Crossword Puzzle

The name of the Signer whose Picture appears in this puzzle is

The word in the key sentence appearing in this puzzle is

....

HORIZONTAL

1. Identical
3. Iridescent gem
9. One who subdues
10. Pertaining to the nose
12. Border or edge
13. Bet
14. Small rug
16. Literary or musical work
18. Location
19. Strip off
20. Part of the leg
21. Hebrew high priest
22. Organ of hearing
23. Chart
25. Unit of energy
28. Attract, decoy, or entice
29. Depend on
31. Maintain (2nd word in the key sentence from the Declaration of Inde- pendence)
32. Covered colonnade
33. Belief
34. Under whose inspiration did Massachusetts, in 1774, invite all the other colonies to send delegates to a grand Continental Congress?
38. Acorn-bearing tree
39. Country in Asia, east of the Mediterranean side
41. On or toward the left side
43. Nimble
44. Float of logs fastened together

VERTICAL

1. First name of today's Signer of the Declara- tion of Independence
2. Part of to be
3. Call of the cat
4. Epoch
5. Unit
6. Equality
7. Like
8. Thin scale or sheet
9. Wigwam
11. More recent
12. Jump on one leg
15. Mound in golf
17. Caused to glide or slide
18. Long pins used chiefly for fastening meat
23. Tie up or secure a vessel
24. Narrow passageways
26. Reply sharply
27. Exhibit satisfaction
28. Definite article
30. Ox-like beast of Central Asia
34. Atmosphere
35. Period of time
36. Deface
37. Mineral spring
40. Regius Professor (abbr.)
42. Pertaining to

1. Identical
5. Iridescent gem
9. One who subdues
10. Pertaining to the nose
12. Border or edge
13. Bet
14. Small rug
16. Literary or musical work
18. Location
19. Strip off
20. Part of the leg
21. Hebrew high priest
22. Organ of hearing
23. Chart
25. Unit of energy
28. Attract, decoy, or entice
29. Depend on
31. Maintain (2nd word in the key sentence from the Declaration of Independence)
32. Covered colonnade
33. Before
34. Under whose inspiration did Massachusetts, in 1774, invite all the other colonies to send delegates to a grand Continental Congress?
38. Acorn-bearing tree
39. Country in Asia, east of the Mediterranean
41. On or toward the left side
43. Nimble
44. Float of logs fastened together

V E R T I C A L

1. First name of today's Signer of the Declaration of Independence
2. Part of to be
3. Call of the cat
4. Epoch
5. Unit
6. Equality
7. Like
8. Thin scale or sheet
9. Wigwam
11. More recent
12. Jump on one leg
15. Mound in golf
17. Caused to glide or slide
18. Long pins used chiefly for fastening meat
23. Ties up or secures a vessel
24. Narrow passageways
26. Reply sharply
27. Exhibit exultation
28. Definite article
30. Ox-like beast of Central Asia
34. Atmosphere
35. Period of time
36. Deface
37. Mineral spring
40. Regius Professor (abbr.)
42. Pertaining to

FIGURE 29 ▪ *Another "Liberty Crossword" Puzzle. Reprinted by permission of King Features Syndicate, © Copyright 1932, King Features Syndicate, Inc.*

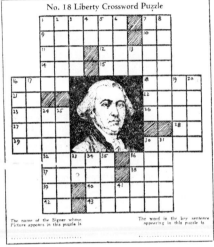

1. Pilfers
7. Printers' measure
9. What Scottish emigrant to the United States, signer of the Declaration of Independence, became associate justice of the Supreme Court in 1793?
10. Exclamation
11. Being; existence
12. Cognomens
14. Devoured
15. Heroic poems
16. Wagers
18. Time
21. Concerning
22. Above
23. Form into a curve
26. Nevada city
27. Roman recruit
28. Part of to be
29. Observes
30. Domesticated
32. Expiate
36. Sin
37. River on which Rome is situated
38. Regret
39. Hebrew word for God
40. Pure silex or flint
42. Prefix, out; from
43. Annoys

1. Exude moisture
2. Shades, colors
3. Otherwise
4. So, thus
5. Solitary
6. Break off short
7. Qualified voter
8. Weighty
13. Note of the musical scale
16. Children; in contemptuous sense
17. Uncanny
19. Colored twilled cotton goods
20. Having a jagged uneven surface
24. Brought into being (12th word in key sentence from the Declaration of Independence)
25. Showing enmity
30. Temporary suspension of hostilities
31. Any open surface (pl.)
33. Great Siberian river
34. Home of a bird
35. One of the Great Lakes
36. The Greek goddess of discord
41. Louisiana (abbr.)

F I G U R E 30 ▪ *An example from* The Celebrities Cross Word Puzzle Book, *which appeared in 1925. The "celebrities" in question didn't actually construct the puzzles, but suggested clues for them. This one is entitled "A Snowflake" and honors Anna Pavlova. The puzzle editor notes: "You would expect Mme. Pavlova, whose exquisite grace is a proverb, to go in for grace in the way of a crossword puzzle design. She has. A very decorative pattern, with a difficult word or two, like several learned, modulating chords between the pretty dance steps of a ballet." Reprinted by permission of Simon and Schuster, a Division of Gulf and Western Corporation.*

H O R I Z O N T A L

1. Contrary (abbr.)
4. Anger
7. Bedouin
9. Suppuration
12. Blemish
13. Kind of lens
15. Spears
17. Remove the seeds of
18. One who testifies under oath
20. Wealthy
22. A type-face (pl.)
23. Enemies of beards
24. Inelegant exclamation
25. Sacred book of Islam
27. Abbr. for liquid measure
28. Flavoring
30. Annoy
31. Governor of Turkish province
33. Individuals
35. Outstanding
38. Short for Alfred
39. Nickel (abbr.)
40. A bone
41. To the (Fr.)

42. Agreements for exchange of prisoners
46. Taking a short sleep
49. Belonging to the lady
50. Goes with bill
52. Trigonometric ratio
53. Calcium, chem. symbol
54. Slice
56. Near
57. Weapon
59. Smoothed out
62. Opposed to anode
63. Rings of light
65. Sweet substance
66. South American mountain range
68. Set of steps
70. Desserts
71. Goddess of the Dawn
72. Narrow opening
73. Crazy
74. Assent

VERTICAL

1. Cereal grass
2. Pointed stick
3. Peeled
4. Sacred images
5. To be bombastic
6. Before
8. Having two poles
9. Preachers
10. Abraham's birthplace
11. Depositing for safe keeping
12. Barren

14. Skeletons of various Anthozoa
15. Pack of cards
16. Nine inches
17. War cry
19. Yes (Sp.)
21. Biblical town
26. Egyptian sun god
28. Word of psalmist
29. Pleasing sounds
31. Loose ends
32. Stupid
33. Moccasin-like shoe
34. Nothing
36. Extinct New Zealand bird
37. Kind of boat
43. Orates
44. Rubbishy
45. Triangle with no two sides equal
46. Beginners
47. Common musical instruments
48. Meanings
51. Alternative conj.
54. Part of musical composition
55. Cupid himself
57. Furnished with glass
58. Toward
60. Correlative of either
61. Day by day
62. Dried leaves of South American shrub
64. Wild European plum
65. Personal pronoun
67. Note of scale
69. Greek letter

The word had, however, already been an entry in the "New Words" section of the 1927 edition. That entry appeared as "cross-word." This recognition was nominal payment for a pastime that had boosted the sale of dictionaries beyond all expectation. (One Christmas issue of *Outlook Magazine* reported a rumor that a new, healthy crop of grass had mysteriously blossomed over the grave of Noah Webster.) At public libraries, dictionaries were deteriorating at an unprecedented rate. The problem grew to such proportions that the industry rallied to address the issue in a 1935 editorial forum in *Library Journal*. Since the average solver did not own an unabridged dictionary, it was only logical that the library serve as a crossword-puzzle contestant's haven. Although libraries were pleased to welcome new patrons, the onslaught had grown unmanageable.

On January 29, 1941 *The Chicago Daily News* reported that 15,000 people had descended upon the Chicago Public Library in a single day—all seeking the answer to the same question! The large number of crossword contests now appearing in the daily press was responsible for increasing library vandalism, as solvers tore out pages containing pertinent words in order to undermine competition. Some kind of standard policy was needed if this type of behavior was to be properly combated.

The Literature and Philology Department of the Los Angeles Public Library offered a "peace plan." In order to better serve both call-in and walk-in requests, the latest reference books were kept by the telephone for easy access, while older editions were scattered liberally throughout the reading room. Those solvers who needed to consult the latest editions were obliged to wait until the telephone queries abated; at that point, they were granted five minutes to find their words. Libraries unable to abide by such policies forbade the use of dictionaries by puzzle contestants. It was proposed that the American Library Association organize a committee for the express purpose of persuading newspapers to work with the libraries by promoting the use of other reference books, thereby taking the strain off the dictionary.

At this time, clues continued to be straight dictionary definitions, using synonyms only. The recurring word "tree" was invariably described by the transparent phrase "woody plant." Any divergence from this system was discouraged. Gelett Burgess openly deplored the use of "smarty-cat" definitions, or clues that were not of the dictionary variety. As a result, the end of the 1930's witnessed a growing indifference to crosswords and such desperate measures on the part of constructors as the creation of "the largest puzzle on earth." Eugene Sheffer was recruited to construct such a monster, which he did with the help of fellow Columbia graduate Walter Gutmann. The oversized grid took two weeks to complete, even with two constructors. In 1938, Robert M. Stilgenbauer of Los Angeles began to work on a gargantuan puzzle that he did not complete until 1949; it contained 2,007 horizontal clues and 2,008 verticals. But these tactics were not enough to help the crossword regain its lost momentum.

It took World War II to restore crosswords to their former prominence, which had, indeed, been partly achieved during World War I. "The boom is on again," declared Mrs. Farrar in the autumn of 1943. The number of solvers had doubled in the preceding twelve months. Every U.S. Army paper included a puzzle for soldiers abroad. One famous anecdote told of two veterans of the Tunisian campaign who worked a puzzle while awaiting orders in a foxhole. Whenever they came across a difficult word they called out for assistance to the soldier in the neighboring foxhole. Astonishingly, he immediately answered all their queries. Later they discovered that he had been reading the answers from a later edition of the newspaper.

But despite the renewed interest in the crossword, *The New York Times* stubbornly refused to provide one for its readers, just as it had throughout the preceding years. In the course of the war, however, publisher Arthur Hays Sulzberger developed an addiction to the crossword puzzle in *The Herald Tribune*, and in 1941 he hired Mrs. Farrar to edit a news-based crossword for *The New York Times* that would reflect the issues of the day. The publisher felt that this additional requirement would provide a puzzle in line with the paper's lofty principles.

From the début puzzle of February 15, 1942 on, *The New York Times* crossword puzzle became the standard by which all American puzzles are measured (Fig. 31). The puzzle first appeared in the Sunday magazine section, and accompanying it was this explanatory note:

> Beginning today, *The New York Times* inaugurates a puzzle page. There will be two puzzles each Sunday—one with a flavor of current events and general information, and one varied in theme, ranging from puzzles in a lighter vein, like today's smaller one, to diagramless puzzles of a general nature.

With World War II blanketing the headlines, the solemn nature of news items was just not compatible with the frivolous nature of the crossword. So Mrs. Farrar began to sneak in general topics with more entertainment value.

The news-oriented crosswords opened up a whole new area by their use of proper names and places; soon celebrities' names were a commonplace,

F I G U R E 31 ▪ *The first* New York Times *Sunday crossword from February 15, 1942 by Charles Erlenkotter.* © The New York Times, *1942. Reprinted by permission.*

H E A D L I N E S   A N D   F O O T N O T E S

A C R O S S

1. Famous one-eyed general.
7. Resourceful.
11. Middle name of news commentator.
15. Alphabet of 28 letters.
21. Flier lost in Pacific, 1937.
22. Obovoid pome.
23. Equipment of Jack Ketch.
24. Be destroyed.
25. Stops the vent of a cannon.
26. Declaimed.
28. Black Sea naval base.
29. Pullet.
30. Name of 3 successive Pharaohs.
32. Italian poet laureate (1544–95)
34. Near East country (abbr.)
35. Before.
36. Fetishes.
37. Rumer.
39. Scholarly.
41. Captivating.
44. Inhabitants of Jolo, Philippines.

46. Authenticate.
47. Fry quickly.
48. Passageways.
50. Suffer.
51. Verbal nouns.
54. "Information Please" expert.
55. "I have not — one wink,"—*Cymbeline*
57. Moving crowd.
61. Hostile.
62. Throwing rope.
64. Power used in the *Clermont.*
66. Man's name.
67. Relative speed.
68. Hundredth of a frame.
70. Native Hindu in British Army.
72. Mr. Whitney, inventor of cotton gin.
73. Lake of which Put-in-Bay is part.
74. Japanese ancestor worship.
76. Went in a circuitous way.
78. Buffalo-nut of China.
80. ½ cent in Japan.
81. "I am — Oracle."
83. Point of mariner's compass.
84. Heedless persons.
87. Designates again.
90. Mouth of a river (Sp.)
93. Hail.
94. G-man Hoover's middle name.
96. Restored.
97. Basket made of rushes.
98. Geneva, in German.
100. Good neighbor.
102. Merest trifle.
103. Spanish watchword.
104. Place in the earth.

106. Early violin.
108. Man's name.
109. Exist in latent style.
110. Turmeric.
112. Review for correction.
114. 50-mile island west of New Guinea.
115. Sacred music.
119. Pertaining to a nobleman.
120. Donald Nelson gives out these.
124. Cobbler's job.
126. Anguillid.
127. Vary.
128. Of age (Latin abbr.)
129. Mastery in works of taste.
130. Gusset.
132. Retaliators.
135. Buy 50 Defense Stamps with this.
136. Wind.
138. Device for indicating speed of blood circulation.
140. Member of Mormon band, "Destroying Angels."
142. Agricultural implement.
143. Moderation.
144. "Men's evil manners — in brass." —*King Henry VIII*
145. Declined.
146. Finishers.
147. Aggrieved.
148. Indefinite quantity.
149. Verbal rhythms.

D O W N

1. Sweeps over.
2. French physicist, student of electrodynamics.
3. Variegated.
4. Member of B.P.O.E.
5. Stead.
6. Weariness.
7. Confirm.
8. Heavy wooden mallet.
9. Tutelary gods.
10. Hermes' son.
11. Small particles.
12. Corrupt.
13. Egyptian goddess.
14. Decoration.
15. Marginal note.
16. Sketched lightly again.
17. Hundred square meters.
18. Dark brown color.
19. What the Treasury does to bonds.
20. Beetlike vegetables.
27. Come back.
31. Compiles.
33. Embroider.
38. Combats.
40. Record.
42. Arrogators.
43. Strait between Nova Scotia and Cape Breton.
44. Dealer named for open stall, his original shop.
45. Proofreader's marks.
48. Noise of distant musketry.
49. Prime necessity for war production.
51. Seaway.
52. "What, never? Hardly—."
53. Having irregular action.

Clues to Figure 31 continue on page 112. **1 1 1**

54. Reluctant allies of Germany.
56. Lessened gradually.
58. Out of a ship.
59. Mouse-like rodent.
60. Poetical ideal of wifely devotion.
62. Brazilian monetary unit.
63. What Damon was to Pythias (Fr.)
65. Fly-by-nights.
68. Platter for meat.
69. Highly important.
71. Pronoun.
74. Potatoes.
75. Inorganic substance.
77. Symbol of appeasement.
79. Take off.
82. Fruit of the mountain ash.
84. Seaport of Honshu Island.
85. Sterilizing apparatus.
86. Showing more normal judgment.
88. Of the (Fr.)
89. Prepare by working.
91. Adduce.
92. Pertaining to the armpit.
95. Invested.
97. Overthrow.
99. Iron prow of gondola.
101. Musical stage production.
103. Port on Zuider Zee, occupied by Nazis.
105. Appreciator.
107. Guide.
109. Scorch.
111. Surveying telescopes.
113. Birthplace of Nathaniel Hawthorne.
114. Of mixed origin.
115. English poet (1754–1832).
116. Illinois town, scene of strike massacre.
117. Nazi submarine base in Belgium.
118. Rank in the Navy (abbr.).
120. Woolen fabric.
121. Naval base in Luzon.
122. Vacillate.
123. War-horses.
125. Suggested Nazi name.
127. Fasten again.
131. Aaron Burr's daughter.
133. Open country in Transvaal.
134. Know.
137. Town in Netherlands.
139. Spike.
141. Spirit worshiped in Thailand.

and many famous people found themselves "among the Ups and Downs," a kind of free publicity that was said to equal one week's free room and board in the Hall of Fame.

The New York Times introduced its Sunday puzzle page with two large crosswords. The news-oriented puzzle, "Headlines and Footnotes" by Charles Erlenkotter, dealt with the educational aspect of the game. Beneath this crossword appeared the whimsical "Riddle Me This" by Anna Gram; if the pseudonym did not sufficiently indicate its humor the editor added this short explanation: "Here are puns and persiflage, anagrams and homonyms, all fair game for the amateur sleuth."

"Puns & Anagrams," as this new style of crossword came to be known, was the brainchild of Alfred Morehead, a bridge columnist at *The New York Times*. Morehead had become captivated by the cryptic crossword while attending a bridge tournament in England. By combining the American style diagram (where all the letters key into two words) with clever and pun-filled clues, Morehead came up with this crossword hybrid. He collaborated with Jack Luzzatto, and together they composed some "Puns & Anagrams" for *Redbook* magazine. Mrs. Farrar chose to include this witty new type of puzzle in *The Times* repertoire, where it found a permanent home.

By March of 1943 a feature article in *The Times* Sunday magazine section discussed this new type of specialization. Whereas the old-fashioned crossword was best tackled in silence with the aid of a strong library, "Puns & Anagrams" soon became a party favorite. The reporter speculated that perhaps wartime breeds insanity, thus explaining the popularity of this offbeat puzzle. A thoroughly banal word like "proffer" would result from the clue "faculty member becomes tender"; a nut became a "screwy kernel." The most commendable aspect of the "Puns & Anagrams" puzzle lay in "making sure that life remains, in the midst of its many gloomy realities, both punny and funny."

At this time Mrs. Farrar devoted herself to editing rather than constructing puzzles, for which she relied on a stable of constructors ranging from a nineteen-year-old student to a freighter captain. Publisher Arthur Sulzberger himself collaborated with editor Charles Merz on several occasions. Legions of housewives and teachers tried their hand at construction. One wealthy Texan cattleman went so far as to employ a full-time secretary to do his research and type definitions. Two of the best and most experienced constructors were Eugene Sheffer and Jack Luzzatto, both of whom had been setting puzzles since their schooldays in the 1920's.

Dividing her time between family life (three children, a husband and a dog) and her crossword commitments (*The New York Times*, the Simon and Schuster volumes, which she edited single-handedly from 1948 until 1978, and army publications), Mrs. Farrar provided the country and its armed forces with welcome distraction during wartime; one U.S. Navy supply ship in appreciation elected her their pin-up girl. But simultaneously she was refining the crossword and exploring its potential. During her early years at *The Times*, she devised new guidelines for constructors. One of her first actions was to banish the two-toed sloth (ai) as well as all other two-letter creatures. The motley crossword zoo (anoa, roc, emu, gnu) was put out to pasture. Her general criteria stipulated that a puzzle be written in good taste, without trade names or diseases, and with a minimum of clichés (Fig. 32). She edited words that violated these boundaries; whereas *The Herald Tribune* allowed the use of the word "urine" (a "perfect" crossword term in that it consists of vowel-consonant-vowel) she adhered to the motto "good news preferred."

Collaborating informally with pioneering constructors, Mrs. Farrar permitted innovations in the puzzles. With the increase of travel, foreign words became both more acceptable and lent an added dimension to the crossword. Common abbreviations provided a real service in the three-letter category. She also limited the number of black squares to one-sixth of the puzzle, creating a more extensive interlock. Jack Luzzatto elaborated on this rule by constructing a crossword with a minimum of black squares.

Before long, the modern, challenging *New York Times* crossword seduced solvers away from standard puzzles like those in *The Herald Tribune*. As all manner of experimental puzzles flooded the pages of *The New York Times*, many people lost interest in the crossword that consisted of nothing but synonyms. In 1943 *Good Housekeeping* reported that "almost anything goes in crosswords today."

The initial topical-news theme gave rise to more fanciful categories; soon themes of all types appeared. This new strategy unified the puzzle by including several longer entries, all joined by a common thread. According to Mrs. Farrar's files, the first constructor to branch out in this direction was advertising executive Harold T. Bers. One of his early "inner-clue" puzzles played on the theme of cats, implied in its title "catalogue." Related terms included pussyfoot, kittenish, caterwaul. This opened up many new possibilities, as definitions were replaced with more whimsical clues. Solvers were forced to think in a new way. "We take every opportunity to add some puzzlement to the crossword by the use of puns or phrasing," confessed Mrs. Farrar. "I can find a funnier definition of 'bulge' than 'World War II battle.' "

According to a *Good Houskeeping* interview with John Farrar, the "Queen of Crosswords" generally started her work after the children had been sent to bed at ten o'clock. She then examined clues and diagrams for typographical errors or improvements until the wee hours. Farrar felt that to accomplish these tasks she required the sort of tranquillity that could be attained only after the city went to sleep. On occasion, he even indulged in a bit of crossword construction himself (one of his efforts appears in the celebrity anthology). Using every available moment, Mrs. Farrar often rode the bus to the office with a stack of puzzles in her lap, each one of which had to be test-solved before it was printed. Fellow passengers came to recognize her and took this unusual opportunity to pick their crossword bones with her.

Ever since the early days, Mrs. Farrar had been a firm believer in audience feedback; she always considered a serious suggestion. In the preface to the 1949 collection of *New York Times* crossword puzzles, she wrote, "Our gratitude goes to the many correspondents who have sent either bouquet or brickbat." Without this constant input, the crossword puzzle would have never left the drawing board at *The World*.

One of the greatest innovations of the 1940's *Times* puzzles was the use of phrases as single entries. This technique is said to have been introduced by New York City school administrator Eugene T. Maleska, a puzzle constructor since the mid-1930's. In one of his puzzles he used the term "hard-shell crab" as an answer, a perfectly legitimate phrase easily found in any dictionary, inspired in his case by an experience clamming on Cape Cod. This brainstorm was included among the spate of puzzles he produced that summer when he realized that he could earn more money as a constructor than as a camp counselor. His new technique offered a rich alternative to the repeated words that plagued the puzzle; Mrs. Farrar ran the clue with the parenthetical indication "two words." As solvers grew accustomed to the innovation, she dropped the hint. "Why should we baby these folks?" she asked. Maleska went on to develop the idea into the "Stepquote," which first appeared in *The New York Times* Sunday magazine in 1964, as a citation that begins at the top left-hand corner of the puzzle and wanders to the bottom right-hand corner. This puzzle caused such a stir that one doctor appealed to Mrs. Farrar for advance answers, since his nurses were too preoccupied to work. It wasn't the first time that she had given away answers. A Columbia University student had once

B E L I E V E   I T   O R   N O T

The strange beast at 61 Across is to be found in Webster's Unabridged, his name an arbitrary coinage described as "quasi New Latin."

A C R O S S

1 Metal stand for holding hot coffee cups, in the Levant
5 Nutritious substance
11 Shaped piece of metal
15 Feature of Spanish architecture

16 Historic town in Burma
17 Seventh word of Genesis
19 Manila hemp plant
20 Under the most favorable circumstances
21 Arm of the Pacific

23 Nickname of a sovereign
24 ——— National Park, in Montana
26 Languish: Poet.
28 Well-known first name in the theatre
29 The Wild Huntsman
31 Instrument for early guided missiles

32 Tropical herb whose fruits are called dishcloth gourds

33 First American to circumnavigate the globe, 1787–90

34 800-mile river into the Irtish

36 Lucian's metamorphosis, in 2nd cen. satire

37 Opera hat

38 Group of retired statesmen, advisers of Japanese emperors

39 An instance of convincing

41 Caprice

42 A size of paper, 12½ × 15 in.

43 E. C. Bentley's detective

44 Infinitive for "catch"

46 Transportation route

49 ——— generis (unique)

50 Phenomena of Angkor Wat

51 Ceremonial forms and courtesies of official life

52 Away from: Prefix

55 Darted: Colloq.

57 Care: Fr.

58 Jaeger

59 Pound into powder

61 Imaginary beast with legs on one side longer than the other, for walking around steep hillsides

63 ——— stitch, called also *petit point*

64 A fiasco: Colloq.

65 Native of France: Abbr.

66 Having a high old time

69 Initials of a famous poet

70 Attribute of a portrait of Satan

72 Really

73 Part of a word: Abbr.

75 Novices: Slang

76 Move or pass slowly

77 East Indian dodder plants

80 Wins a card game

81 ——— -ums, biting insects

82 "Puss ———"

84 After: Fr.

86 English satirist, collaborated with Marlowe

87 Native of Dahomey

89 Small northern constellation

90 The rigging of a ship

91 Lord Herbert was its "father"

92 Rich silk cloth of the Middle Ages

94 ——— Ghazi Khan, Punjab province of Pakistan

95 Originally, a counterfeit Irish halfpenny

96 Composer of "Huckleberry Finn"

97 In a great hurry

99 Noun suffix meaning "small"

100 River of Hades

102 From that time

104 Cobra on the headdress of ancient Egyptian rulers

106 Driver of a golden chariot

107 Highly irritable person

108 ——— tree, the whitewood

109 Part of a watermelon

110 Well-known name in baseball

111 Equipment for certain troops

D O W N

1 Where cloves come from

2 ——— loss (puzzled)

3 Source of Alberich's magic

4 Young animals

5 A gentle slope

6 Spaniards

7 Turkic dweller in Asia

8 Wild beast: Comb. form

9 Followed by 12 Down, a skating rink

10 Pretty good

11 Home of the prophet Amos

12 Highway: Ger.

13 Coin of Macao

14 Tourist's investment

15 Released, as a rope

17 Characteristic of the Ungulata

18 Designation of a spectral type

19 Designs used in the Rorschach test

22 Ring decision

25 Presidential middle name

27 Creator of Barney Greenwald

30 Count ———

32 Mortgages

Clues to Figure 32 continue on page 118.

33 Slangy invitation to depart

35 Dr. Pauling, Nobel prize winner in chemistry, 1954

37 Range of cliffs in central Washington

38 British general, hero of Malta

40 Producing: Suffix

41 Coachmen

42 The color peacock blue

44 Historic capital of Champagne

45 ———— home

46 Decisive event, in France

47 1 and 5 Across, for instance

48 Not downcast

51 Breed of pigeon

52 Commander of Saul's army

53 Peak in Utah, 11,054 ft.

54 Scholar who writes lives of the saints

56 Blunderbore and others

57 Dignity and pomp

60 Describing certain cake mixtures

62 Act in concert

65 Passes, in sports

67 "Wise ———— owl"

68 "The Peanut Vendor"

71 German number

72 Island of Iran, in Strait of Hormuz

74 Oslo ————

76 A dimple

78 Namesakes of Anita Loos heroine

79 Accumulate

81 Childlike

82 Something that is FYI

83 Clouts

84 Akbar's capital, 1566

85 Clingstone

86 Airplane beacons

87 Wealthy person from whom large political campaign contributions are expected: Slang

88 Threatens or attempts

91 Hero of 1870 novel

92 Short narrative

93 Months of French calendar

96 Expression of the "little crocodile"

97 Chervil

98 Group of volcanic islands, West Pacific

101 Man's name meaning "high"

103 Book of the Old Testament: Abbr.

105 Fabled woodcutter

requested advance answers in order to get into a fraternity that required the successful completion of the Sunday puzzle. In order not to violate crossword rules, Mrs. Farrar supplied only hints to the desperate student. Another student approached Mrs. Farrar for some solutions because she was dating a crossword aficionado whom she wanted to impress. Mrs. Farrar revealed the answers, hoping as she did so that she had not saddled a bright young man with a scheming vixen.

A third Maleska suggestion was the institution of a daily *New York Times* puzzle. The first one appeared on September 11, 1950, on the book page. Its placement caused unforeseen conflict; a disgruntled husband complained that while he enjoyed reading the editorial page, his wife looked forward to the puzzle on the reverse side. A tussle would generally ensue over who got first dibs on the page. This issue was upsetting an otherwise ideal twenty-four-year marriage. Could the management please move the puzzle? Mrs. Farrar suggested that the couple buy two newpapers and contribute one to a nearby hospital.

By this time, educational experts had begun to see the crossword as a vocabulary builder. Only an estimated 3,000 English words are commonly used in standard communication. Crosswords extended these limits. However, as poet Phyllis McGinley put it in a 1953 *New York Times* article, this was of secondary importance to solvers. "Who wants education with the morning cup of coffee or on a quiet Sunday afternoon?" All the solver hopes for is a "gentle brain jog."

Once *The New York Times* shifted the focus of solving away from the dictionary, reliance on reference books became suspect. Solving was a challenge to one's innate wit rather than a research exercise. And puzzles began to be written on every level, from grade school up. With the beginning of the 1950's, it became clear the crosswords had developed into a tradition. Marlene Dietrich admitted to her weakness for the little squares; Churchill was reported to have almost missed a cabinet meeting while wrestling with a particularly stubborn clue. Author Jean Stafford confessed that she would have thought more highly of herself if she began the day translating instead of solving. In 1954 Princess Margaret entered a crossword contest held by *Country Life* and came out with first prize! When the judges read her name on the entry blank, they questioned its veracity, but the secretary to the Princess confirmed that indeed it was the work of her employer. "All the royal family are very keen on crosswords," she revealed, "but this is the first time any one of them has won a puzzle contest."

Yet despite all the publicity, crossword popularity waned in the decade after World War II. Discouraged by poor attendance at the 1957 National Puzzlers' League convention, the officials canceled future gatherings, which were not reconvened until 1976. Again, a change of pace was called for. David Cort, self-avowed "crossword addict," recorded his objections in *The Nation* in the summer of 1961. One possible reason for the sagging challenge, he theorized, was the paltry rates paid to constructors. *The New York Times* offered $10 for a daily 15 × 15 square puzzle and a whopping $25 for the Sunday jumbo (21 × 21 or 23 × 23). If the best American puzzles paid so poorly, there was little hope for the future. Another hindrance was the tiresome cliché that could not be shaken. "As the closets of the mind fill up with this rubbish, one may be troubled by one's inability to forget it all, to forget sil and elater, and ret and tor and adit and seesee or ort and alb," Cort added. Yet dictionaries and encyclopedias were full of intriguing terms that had never appeared in crossword form.

The only glimmer of hope that Cort saw lay in the British-style puzzles, where the commonplace word "oceanic" could be defined not as "pertaining to a large body of water," but perhaps as "cocaine mixture" to indicate an anagram. Cort rhapsodized on the fiendish cryptic puzzle of the London *Observer*. Although his sentiments did not affect the general solving public, his proposals were not as far-fetched as they might have seemed; within the next decade a small but stalwart movement would adapt the cryptic to American taste.

When *The New York Times* asked Mrs. Farrar to retire in 1969 at the age of seventy-two, the management had no idea how strongly solvers would respond. (The mandatory retirement age is seventy, but since she was not a reporter, Mrs. Farrar managed to slip past the rules for two years.) By this time the public had grown dependent on her good judgment to provide them with worthwhile puzzles; generations of solvers had been weaned on her work. Cries of outrage sounded from every part of the country at the news of her departure. Odes were created in honor of the single most important figure in the evolution of the American crossword puzzle. To separate the crossword from Mrs. Farrar's capable hands was unthinkable. *New Yorker* writer E. J. Kahn addressed a letter to the editor in which he expressed the feelings of countless commuting solvers:

> I am one of the people whose lives Margaret Farrar has ruined. For nearly twenty
> years, when I lived in Westchester, I took part in a spirited competition on the

commuter train to see who could finish the daily puzzle first. The rule was that you couldn't even peek at it until the train started to move out of 125th Street on its way to Grand Central—an eleven-minute trip . . . And because of all the happy hours I have spent as [Mrs. Farrar's] disciple, I cannot let her retirement go by without expressing my fervent appreciation for all the challenging pleasure she has given me.

In truth, a replacement was hard to find. Baffled by this predicament, the *New York Times* Sunday editor Daniel Schwarz scouted the in-house possibilities. The only name that came to his attention was that of Will Weng, head of the *Times*'s metropolitan copy desk. A few years earlier, Weng had created a crossword on the theme of Joe Miller jokes; he was also a contributor to the crossword magazines published by Dell. With these credentials, Weng was recruited to take over Mrs. Farrar's exalted post. Since she had the flu at the time, it was urgent that he assume the position at once and forfeit a vacation. As a result, Weng embarked on his new career without the advantage of a training period; using the comprehensive guidelines that Mrs. Farrar had carefully prepared, he set to work.

The initial response was predictably hostile. How could an "intruder" dare to trespass on hallowed ground? Author Jean Stafford remarked in *Esquire* that "since the departure of the meticulous and honorable Mrs. Farrar, [the puzzle's] creators have picked up so many offensive linguistic habits from the airwaves and from Presidential speech writers that they should be ashamed of themselves." The irony in this was that Weng was following Mrs. Farrar's instructions to the letter, and some of the puzzles that were criticized had been completely edited by Mrs. Farrar before her retirement. Daniel Schwarz defended Weng throughout the siege, and after six months solvers adjusted to the new regime. Words of encouragement gradually tempered the vehement letters as Weng began to formulate new policies.

During the first months Weng had allowed many of the regular constructors to do as they pleased; after all, he reasoned, they had created the business. But once he graduated from "interloper" to peer, he began to assert his powers. Besides, the rules governing the American crossword had always been flexible. Weng soon realized that he would have to build on the foundation he had inherited by putting his own stamp on the crossword puzzle. He began to open up new avenues of growth, injecting more wit and humor into the puzzles. His first year in office had been characterized by a defensive approach, "keeping my neck out of the guillotine," as he put it; thereafter things were different (Fig. 33).

POUND FOR POUND

Dieting can be a lonely chore. Maybe this will keep you company.

ACROSS

1. Punish with a fine
7. Swung around
12. Neckwear decor
18. One's life work
19. New Orleans' Vieux ———
20. Of no difference
21. What some people get when they study the scales
23. Mortar's partner
24. Road curve
25. River of France
26. Seance noises
28. Showed the way
29. Miss Doone
30. Certain contract
32. River islands
33. Burns's sweet river
36. Food for people who like to cram things
39. Desserts
40. Cake frosting ornament
42. Miss Davis
45. Dance
47. Pronoun
48. Put on ———, as a baseball player
50. Echoed
52. Complete
54. New York canal
55. Places in a store where rich foods are sold
59. U.S. publisher
61. Famed jockey
62. Virginia willow
63. Rood and tau
65. Mountain of Crete

67. Airline board listing
72. Kitchen gadget
73. Capacity
75. Verne captain
76. A boaster's potbelly, in a way
79. Ahead
80. Social group
82. Musical work
83. Cuckoopints
86. Indefinite degree
87. Adjective suffix
88. Vacant
89. Fattening beverage
92. Eat like ———
94. Generalized scale readings for the overweight
98. Child's garment
99. Problem for a vet
100. Flair
101. Spots
102. Old chariot
103. Lawyer's concern

D O W N

1. Head or heart ailment
2. Miss West and others
3. Geological times
4. Gun up the engine
5. Island off India
6. Mistake
7. Egyptian images
8. Put on cargo
9. Swiss canton
10. Sea bird
11. Bring into dishonor
12. Machine lever
13. French islands
14. City transport lines
15. Overtight belts of fat men, so to speak
16. Waterway
17. Requires
22. One: Ger.
27. Domestic beast
29. Dieter's triumph
30. What two overweight people might say and then go on
31. ——— excess
32. Run ——— (be ill)
33. Army address
34. Five-spot
35. Golf-ball perch
37. Defendants, in Roman law
38. Where, to Caesar
40. Tranquillity
41. "Salome" and "Aida"
43. Numerical prefix
44. Compass reading
46. Indian cymbals
48. Attacked
49. Main road
51. Clamor
53. Black bird of New Zealand
55. Sounds that bode ill for the scales
56. Declare
57. Nondieter's favorite kind of thing
58. Attention
59. Month: Abbr.
60. Shout: Fr.
64. Sign for a hit show
66. Jolson and others
68. Stopping places
69. Fido's M.D.
70. ———, amas, amat
71. Trim
73. "———, the deluge"
74. Like a solitaire game
77. Earth pigments
78. U.S. money unit: Abbr.
79. Greek letters
80. Trap
81. Habits of a group
84. British heroes of W.W. II
85. Merge
87. "——— a man in your future"
88. U.S. playwright
89. Length times width
90. Seasonal time
91. Italian family
93. Campus in Troy, N.Y: Abbr.
95. Western group: Abbr.
96. Us: Ger.
97. Business letter abbr.

First of all, he decided to quash the "Bermuda onion" school of crossword construction—the early 1950's custom of featuring clues that combined countries and foods in what had originally seemed a clever manner. As a result, Brussels sprouts, French toast and Molotov cocktails soon went the way of gnu and emu. Equally hackneyed were colors: Blue Danube, Red China and Black Forest. Weng banished them from *Times* crosswords, along with "Ernest Hemingway," *The Sun Also Rises* and *A Farewell to Arms*, three entries that, because they have fifteen letters each, were ideal thematic entries since they reached across the daily 15×15 puzzle grid and, as a result, appeared more often than any other single theme.

Although Weng added more humor to the standard American crossword, he did not subscribe to the bizarre humor characteristic of the British puzzle. Unable to work cryptics himself, he characterized them as a "pointless exercise with a perverted sense of humor." He never allowed a cryptic to appear on the *New York Times* puzzle page, and in retrospect, he considered this his greatest achievement as puzzle editor.

Under his aegis, the Sunday puzzle became an experimental vehicle in which words read backwards or vowels were excluded, and all manner of silly variations were tested (Fig. 34). Weng encouraged light-hearted experimentation, such as the replacement of words with symbols in crossword answers. His premise was that the crossword was a game and as such should be fun; he saw no educational merit whatsoever in solving. "Who can remember a word out of context?" he asked. He admitted that even as a constructor he was constantly rechecking to make sure that his memory had not failed him.

Before long, solvers became accustomed to Weng's freewheeling style. Parenthetical aids were discarded; the clue itself indicated the route to take. An answer such as "alts" could be indicated with the term "hts." instead of "heights (abbr.)." In addition to a core of regular contributors, Weng used many "one-shot" constructors—housewives, retired educators, priests, accountants, lawyers and film people—who worked on a single inspiration. Although he did receive an occasional crossword from two convicts in the Ohio Penitentiary in Columbus, Weng found the belief that prisoners make expert constructors an old wives' tale. (Jack Luzzatto has reported that he too received crosswords from the same prison while editing for *Magazine Management* in the late 1960's, but he soon discovered that one of his prison contributors was plagiarizing from one of Luzzatto's own early works by copying the diagram and doctoring the clues.)

Like his predecessor, Weng tried to test-solve every puzzle, although an occasional typographical error escaped his scrutiny. When the word "deed" appeared as "deep" the connecting vertical became "daybep." Several solvers wrote in for a definition of the strange word. (Jack Luzzatto had a similar experience when he wrote "dope" for "Pope" as the answer for the definition "Catholic chief.") Often errors occurred in the composing room, and when *The New York Times* turned from hot to cold type in the late 1970's, the paste-ups sometimes fell off, leaving words without clues.

The most important lesson Weng learned during his eight years as crossword editor was the need for accuracy. The key lay in test-solving and thereby checking every detail, but on rare occasions he relied on his memory, as in the case of one puzzle that featured mixed drinks. A grasshopper was defined as a vodka drink; subsequently his office received reams of recipes from more experienced bartenders. When John Glenn was described as the first earth orbiter, a solver asked: "How would you define Yuri Gagarin?" And when, in an effort to recycle the tired answer "tepee," Weng used the clue "Home for Powhatan," a Princeton scholar wrote to explain that only Plains Indians lived in tepees, and Powhatan was from Delaware. Mrs. Farrar found her memory equally unreliable. She once defined Captain Ahab as the owner of a wooden leg; an eight-year-old boy brought her down a peg by informing her that he had a leg of whalebone.

Time and time again Weng was taken to task in the game of one-upmanship between puzzle editor and solver. Sometimes solvers demanded explanations even when there was no error. In one such case, Weng used the clue "970 Down" to represent the answer "misnumber." Indignant solvers were quick to report the "misprint."

When Will Weng, having reached his seventieth birthday, was asked to retire in 1977, he anticipated the same sort of fuss that had attended the retirement of Mrs. Farrar eight years earlier. In order to minimize the transitional uproar, he took it upon himself to name a successor, selecting Eugene Maleska from among the top ranks of old-time constructors. Maleska had dabbled in crosswords since his school days at Montclair State College in New Jersey. Some of his earliest efforts were labors of love in honor of his future bride Jean, whose name was regularly defined as "Best-looking girl on campus." She was so proud of these unusual valentines that she showed them to her roommate, who suggested that the constructor try for a wider market. *The Herald Tribune* in New York finally accepted a Maleska puzzle in 1934—after at least forty rejections. (Soon after this

FIGURE 34 ▪ *This crossword, "It's Suitable," by Jo Paquin, King Features puzzle editor and constructor since 1940, illustrates Weng's influence in the field. It was published on May 14, 1978. Average time of solution: 75 minutes. Reprinted by permission of King Features Syndicate, © Copyright 1979 King Features Syndicate, Inc.*

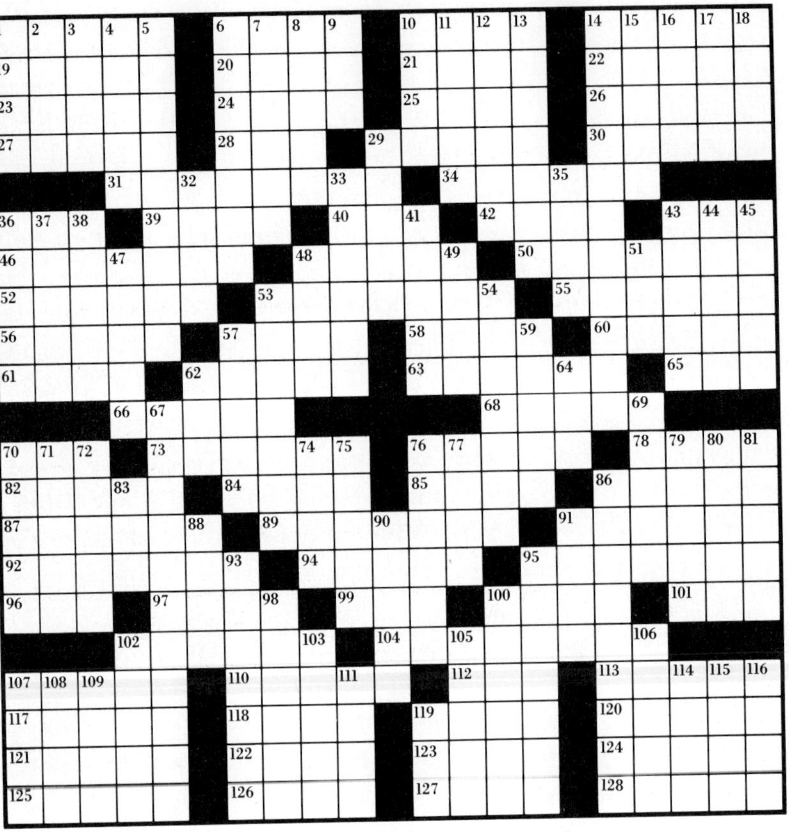

ACROSS

1 Famous gem
6 Prescription unit
10 Of the ear
14 Digestive distress
19 Hiroshima's downfall
20 Grafted (Her.)
21 Ship: Jap.
22 Misrepresent
23 Machine part
24 Asterisk
25 Minute particle
26 GWTW hero
27 Noted hostess
28 Russian plane
29 Dried plum
30 Alleviates
31 Kind of blastomere
34 Middle
36 Weight, in India
39 ———— Kleine Nachtmusik
40 And others (abbr.)
42 Skater's area
43 Articles
46 Warbled
48 City in Florida
50 Live together
52 More risqué
53 Deli items
55 Legal minority
56 ———— in the dark
57 "———— Death"
58 Dashiell Hammett character

60 Sheer
61 Hammer part
62 Choral composition
63 Delectable crustaceans
65 Sooner than
66 Very unhappy
68 Gave special color to
70 Limited (abbr.)
73 Turkic hordes
76 Bizarre
78 Yeans
82 Vegetable caterpillar
84 Related
85 Journey by ox wagon
86 Medical problem
87 Asocial ones
89 Worker in Pittsburgh
91 Site of Roma
92 Generous repast
94 Inventor Howe
95 Idolater
96 Draft org.
97 Hawk parrots
99 Statute
100 Bridge bid
101 Bishop's diocese
102 Exercising volition
104 Ripen
107 Dress designer
110 Marsh grasses
112 Equal: comb. form
113 Soap plant
117 Seed coats
118 Far: comb. form
119 Pro ———
120 Book (Lat.)
121 French security
122 Ireland
123 Angered
124 ——— lights
125 Spanish houses

126 A groom, in India
127 Defaces
128 Installs

D O W N

1 Injure
2 Orchestral instrument
3 Kitchen items
4 Ham it up
5 Expensive gift
6 Irish earldom
7 Early
8 Phase
9 Poet's word
10 Sharif
11 Actress O'Neal
12 Household appliance
13 Pertaining to comedy
14 Play by George
    Bernard Shaw
15 Irish playwright
16 Rubber trees
17 Ceremony
18 Seines
29 Flower organ
32 A row
33 Form again
35 Privy to
36 Leather thong
37 Obliterate
38 Nouveau ———
41 To embrace
43 Lessen
44 African river
45 Cubic meter
47 Richard I
48 Hosea (N.T.)
49 City in Judah
51 Hill-builder

53 Menu items
54 To dabble in
57 Large artery
59 Preliminary drudgery
62 Extinct bird
64 Compass reading
67 Magazines
69 Transfer pattern
70 Refrains in songs
71 Raise for 100 Across
72 Patron saint of France
74 Hoarfrost
75 Short fishing line
76 Canadian capital
77 Mists (Scot.)
79 West ———,
    Wisconsin
80 Clamor
81 Declare
83 Egyptian sun god
86 Intimate conversations
88 Navigate
90 O'Flaherty, et al.
91 Notion
93 Father of Odysseus
95 Forays
98 Disdainful
100 Wrongful
    dispossession
102 Italian physicist
103 Purposive
105 Coronet
106 Author Zola
107 Park (Fr.)
108 Region
109 Containers
111 English sand hill
114 Obeah (var.)
115 Manor court (Hist.)
116 Work units
119 Edge

success, *The Herald Tribune* bought the rejections.) Eventually—and after making some minor adjustments—Mrs. Farrar bought Maleska's work for *The New York Times*. From that time on she acted as Maleska's mentor; their partnership was formalized in 1978 when she asked Maleska to coedit the Simon and Schuster series with her. Maleska traded one career for another: he embarked on his career as *New York Times* crossword editor just as he stepped down from his post as assistant superintendent of schools in the Bronx.

When Maleska assumed his new responsibilities in 1977, Weng warned him about the possibility of negative reader reaction. The new regime began with some adjustments to puzzle construction: Maleska reduced the number of words in the daily puzzle from 78 or 80 to 76, thereby creating larger islands of interlocking letters and limiting the number of three-letter words. Humor was retained although modified; as an educator Maleska reinstated a more academic tone. Whereas Weng rewrote about half the clues in any given puzzle, Maleska tended to rewrite about three-quarters. At his Cape Cod retreat, he worked twelve-hour days, seven days a week, accepting puzzles months in advance of their appearance. With the help of his wife and an extensive reference collection, he prepared the puzzles for publication. Of an estimated five hundred contributions, he found only one-third acceptable; and even these were tailored to his rules. Solvers objected to the solemn turn the puzzles were taking while constructors (now more formally known as "cruciverbalists") complained about heavy editing. Maleska defended his position by claiming that he was a "middle-of-the-road" editor between the traditional and cryptic factions.

In a 1974 Gallup poll it was reported that there were an estimated thirty million crossword-puzzle-solvers in the United States; and toward the end of the decade the puzzle was showing increased vigor. In 1978, *Games* magazine was launched, with a circulation of 200,000 for the first issue. "We stepped into a highly energized vacuum," commented managing editor Michael Donner. The same year an annual crossword marathon, sponsored by the Hemming-Hulburt Booksellers in Beachwood, Ohio, was introduced. The grand prize was $1,000 for the first successfully completed diagram. The event took place in the bookstore itself, and contestants had twenty-four hours to complete the puzzle with free run of all the reference works at hand. Twenty-three hours later, *Games* editor Donner, having solved 88 percent of the crossword, emerged victorious and claimed the $1,000 first prize. The puzzle, set by Jordan Lasher, was so difficult that many potential contestants left after scanning the clues. For the 1979 contest, the sponsors requested Lasher to simplify his definitions. This time *Games* associate editor Will Shortz—an illustrious constructor in his own right—walked away with the prize in a cool nine hours.

Shortz was no newcomer to the crossword-contest revival; in 1977 he had helped coordinate the annual American Crossword Puzzle Tournament in Stamford, Connecticut. This three-day event, beginning on Friday night with an informal introduction to Margaret Farrar and other crossword celebrities, includes two rounds of puzzles on Saturday and a championship play-off on Sunday (Figs. 35 and 36). Each contestant fills in seven crosswords, which are then scored for accuracy and speed, and the affair concludes with an awards banquet at which cash prizes are presented to the three top solvers.

In 1980, a new touch was added: for the last round the three finalists raced to solve a crossword which was projected behind them on three screens for the benefit of the audience. Of the 120-odd contestants, twenty-nine-year-old Department of Defense mathematician Daniel L. Pratt made off with the $300 first prize. The 1979 incumbent, Miriam Raphael, a schoolteacher, came in second, followed by Joel Darrow, a banking house portfolio manager. The three winners agreed that the decisive crossword ("Anything Goes" by Jordan Lasher) was extremely difficult. One clue that stumped all of them was 19 Across: "Tale of a desert youth as an agent?" (Answer: Gobi teen.)

Pratt attributed his success to a lifelong addiction to Scrabble® combined with intensive reading in science. Surprisingly, he was not a daily solver. To prepare for the tournament he had practiced by working out half a puzzle book.

To the pioneers in the field, the crossword revival of the 1970's recalled the craze of 1924. In 1974, the golden anniversary of that momentous year, crossword constructors from all over the country gathered in New York City to honor the woman who had played such an important role in all their lives: Margaret Farrar. Since her retirement from *The Times* in 1969, Mrs. Farrar had become crossword editor for *The Los Angeles Times*. In a *New York Times* "guest word" article in the Sunday book section on April 7, 1974, she observed that for all her years of devotion to the crossword, her main reward was "a ragbag of words." She was also pleased to observe "the humbling knowledge that 'out there' in the U.S.A. was a heap of solvers, at least twenty million Across and ten million Down."

The success of the luncheon inspired one of the guests to compile a

A C R O S S

1 Tough luck
7 Who said slips are intentional?
12 Composition by Bach, e.g.
13 Lack of discipline
16 Stop sign, for one
17 Hurried, in music
18 Source of strange powers
20 Heraldic wreath
21 Runners?
22 The N in N.B.
23 Luckless Boleyn
24 Gripper
25 Mortise mate
26 Sign up for more
28 Abettors
29 Science of medicine: Comb. form
31 Shock
35 ———— as possible (minimum)
40 Bias

41 Dreadful
42 White-powdered fertilizer
43 Draw ragged breaths
44 Famed New York Sun editor
45 Facing a glacier
46 Where spirits dwell?
49 Fell back
50 Apprentice
51 Loner
52 Alphabetical lists in books
53 Name in furs and lodging
54 Family of composer Julie of "Gypsy"

D O W N

1 First break of the sound barrier
2 Hospital doctor
3 Perennial candidate
4 De facto Netherlands capital
5 Perched on
6 Game show celeb

7 Strengthening rim of a wheel

8 Traditional modes of music from India

9 Disappearing act

10 Full of sour notes

11 Sweetheart

12 Cottage-dwelling peasant

14 Stationary machine part

15 Big white gannets

19 Forcible control

24 Mini bottle

25 "Then 'twas the Roman; now ———" (A.E. Housman)

27 Bouncy tune

28 Hardwood tree of Asia

30 Sabras

31 Aim high

32 Wood shaver

33 Sovereign remedy

34 Country music

36 Give special training to

37 Defeat soundly and roundly

38 Lease parties

39 Givers of relief

41 Irish, when up

44 Owing

45 Bordering on the illegal

47 Underground passage

48 Bucky's depression?

F I G U R E 36 ▪ *"Questionnaire" by Maura Jacobson, the final crossword in the Stamford, Connecticut 1979 American Crossword Puzzle Tournament. The puzzle carries the note: "Diverse inquiries into serious matters." Reprinted by kind permission of the author.*

A C R O S S

1 Talked back
7 Bombay bigwig
12 Extemporize
17 Secondhand
21 ——— time
22 "What's in ———?"
23 See 44 Down
24 Malarial fever
25 What results from embassy vaccinations?
28 Break
29 Wings
30 Airport transportation
31 "——— a man with seven wives"
32 Algonquians
33 Novelist Lagerlöf
35 Moorish drums
38 Guard against
41 Underdog's hope
43 Pat patterns
45 Memo
49 At the bow
51 Alfresco
54 ——— Mochis, Mexico
55 Home of the Copacabana
56 "I love ———"
59 What do New England barbers use?
62 What kind of jam is made in the jungle?
65 Is beholden to

66 Defendant's friend, often
67 Charge
68 Roulette bet
69 Toy bear
71 Popular general
72 Actor Noah
74 What does the Capitol otologist check?
80 Referee's count
81 Fitting
82 Wave: Sp.
83 "Best defenseman" 1968–75
84 Mister
85 What concerns thrifty horses?
90 Collected writings
92 Depot abbr.
93 Actor's quest
94 Brit. cadet school
95 "The Magic Mountain" author
96 Ark groupings, e.g.
97 Primer lore
99 Where do Julius' fans sit?
105 What does Travolta do on the beach?
108 "———, and away!"
109 Scottish single
110 Piston
111 Belgrade native
113 Duck ———
114 Breathes
117 Recite rapidly (with "off")
118 Abalone shell
121 "Be present" in old Rome
123 To ——— (somewhat)
125 Bodily orifices
130 Section in bookbinding

133 Bird life
135 11th century poet
136 Compeer of Dali
137 Samovars
138 When is a touchdown declared?
144 "Must have been something ———"
145 Tuscany city
146 Go-between
147 Kind of mail or object
148 Labor
149 Little brothers
150 Like penicillin
151 Puts forth energy

D O W N

1 Drinks
2 Weak and outdated
3 Modified leaf
4 Hawthorne's birthplace
5 V-mail destination
6 Mother
7 Flightless bird
8 Sprightly, in music
9 Pat's Senate colleague
10 "What a good boy ——— "
11 Take up
12 Astringent substance
13 Star in Cygnus
14 Hang around
15 Bankbk. entry
16 Tunisian ruler
17 Burger or predecessor
18 Sigmoid molding
19 April fool
20 Opponent for Knicks
26 A wail
27 Gaffe
32 Fresh and cold
34 Of the ear
36 Open spaces: L.

37 Sally ——— (teacakes)
39 Sci-fi author
40 Mine, in Caen
42 Start for cure or form
44 West African nation, with 23-Across
46 What did the artistic duelist do?
47 De Valera's land
48 She's Dorothy now
49 What was the result of the bridge collapse?
50 Turkish army corps
52 Fire base
53 Brick facing
56 Is in store for
57 Striker
58 No longer productive
60 Sign over
61 "D"
63 Roasting ———
64 Be nosy
69 Brew, in a way
70 Regatta gear
72 Prom
73 Swordplay
74 Sault Ste. Marie
75 O'Neill tree
76 A rejection
77 "Mad" one
78 Radioactive elements
79 French perfume city
86 Warrant officer
87 Gizzard
88 Signs
89 Khrushchev ally
90 Pallid
91 Switch ups
95 Yucatan Indian
96 Noun suffix
97 Cracked, in a way
98 Kind of china
99 "If Winter ——— . . ."

Clues to Figure 36 continue on page 134. **1 3 3**

100 Side by side
101 Not bare
102 Roman official
103 Meet the challenge
104 The "y" in "ye"
106 "——— of
      Frankenstein"
107 Extraordinary
112 Mabel of the silents
115 Analyzed
116 Avers
119 Homes, e.g.
120 Blackbird: Poetic
122 In any ———
124 Noted comedian
126 Love, in Capri
127 Delta site
128 Like hominids
129 Ilks
130 Jest
131 River or mountains
132 "Come ——— my
      parlor"
134 Times
138 Nile viper
139 Word of reproof
140 Radio man
141 Freudian study
142 Carp's kin
143 Kind of shooter

directory of names and addresses for future gatherings. Father Edward O'Brien's Directory—as it came to be known—was the work of a curate from upstate New York. Beside each name he included short "self-biographies of men and women who share [the] lust for fame and fortune without profit." (By 1978 *The New York Times*, always the standard in the field, was offering $20 for a daily crossword and $100 for a Sunday one.) This modest homemade "Compendium of Cruciverbalists" revealed the spectrum of constructors; professors, interior decorators, playwrights and disc jockeys were among the two hundred-odd respondents. One seasoned cruciverbalist had even made an appearance on an early *What's My Line?* program. "The philosophy that we are a 'family' underlay the communications upon which this directory was formed," Father O'Brien wrote. "Only we know how it feels to conceive and labor over a 15 × 15 brainchild."

Although the directory did not result in any plans for reunions, it did serve to attest to the fact that a crossword community existed in the United States. Across the Atlantic, the Crossword Club mobilized British forces in April of 1978. About six hundred members, including fifty Americans, rallied to promote the cryptic crossword. Among these were some of the great contemporary setters such as "Azed" of the *Observer*, and "Zander," "Centigram," "Mass," "Salamanca" and "Apex," all frequent contributors to *The Listener* (Fig. 37). The American contingent indicated a movement in the United States toward the adoption of the cryptic. After half a century of solving, Americans were beginning to be ready to decipher the British code (Figs. 38 and 39).

FIGURE 37 ▪ *"Crossing the Bar,"* a puzzle by *"Centigram,"* reproduced from Crossword, *the magazine of Britain's "Crossword Club," by kind permission of the editor. It appears with the note: "Definitions are normal, but, taking the title into account, the answer contains one extra letter, at the beginning or the end, separated in the diagram by a bar. E.g., 10 Ac. plus the second letter of 7 Dn."*

ACROSS

1 Old concubine infatuated with a friend (5)

5 Hating marriage, but coming together sexually (7)

10 Mineral, i.e. tango perhaps in ancient vessel (9)

11 Cane tree (4)

12 Such a bid is a gamble, holding queen (6)

14 Garland in a short line produces pungent chemical (8)

15 Fine grating almost containing commotion (6)

17 A job needing two vessels (4)

18 With a small garden tool I paid back a weed (8)

20 Wanton: a party with a certain lively dance (8)

23 One who mentions a family (4)

24 Animals chopped up to make sausage (6)

25 Skunk swallows boring tool—a spray (8)

28 Grow most of the bearded wheat (6)

29 Inclination that is suffered inwardly (4)

30 Silent relic could be this left abandoned on the moon (9)

31 Tangled, according to nature one left in to clear up (7)

32 Threw about a lot in convulsions (5)

DOWN

1 I'll give you a butt with the appropriate weapon (7)

2 Narcotic plant gives a short 'draw'—a pull almost inhaled (6)

3 Eastern lizard, an obscure one turned up in a stone (8)

4 Record broken by a monkey (4)
5 I sanction changes, but I don't produce any (8)
6 Futile movement, without purpose, both beheaded (6)
7 Kind of fruit one has to preserve (4)
8 Picture with movable parts; a huge number love to butt in (9)
9 Once ripped your canvas, top to bottom (5)
13 Monster fish (a young one) swallows a tailless goat—antelope (9)
16 To prevent reversing round unfinished narrow street, it's restricted (8)

17 Eddy puts the reverse of hard clues in to deceive (8)
19 Third? Second after endeavour, we hear, in race (7)
21 Paid, having to split a pound, for rubbish (6)
22 Product of bullet died, almost winged one (6)
23 A stern, possibly (5)
26 Odd guessing game (4)
27 Most of the air splits dry skin (4)

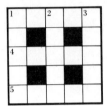

**W A R M U P
P U Z Z L E**

A C R O S S

1 To clean messy curbs (5) *anagram*
4 "Come back, Ron, I'm not yet twenty-one!" (5) *reversal*
5 Change the males in the commercial (5) *container*

D O W N

1 There's a moat concealing an island (5) *concealed word*
2 A stove, to an extent (5) *second definition*
3 Tired of the inn's meals, we hear (5) *homonym*

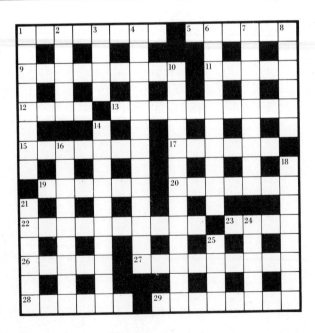

CROSSWORD À L'ANGLAISE

The fun of British crosswords lies in seeing through their tricks. Each clue contains: (1) a definition or direct reference to the answer, and (2) a second description of the answer through wordplay. Look for instructions in the clues to help you. Words suggesting disorder, like "crazy," etc., are telltale signs of anagrams; "back" and "returning" are indicators of reversals; "they say" and "we hear" are signposts for homonyms. *1 Across* is an example of a charade clue. The answer, ANTELOPE ("animal"), splits into two parts (indicated by the words "breaks for"): "the stake" (ANTE) and "an easy gait" (LOPE). (The number of letters in answer words is given in parentheses.)

ACROSS

1 Animal breaks for the stake with an easy gait (8)
5 Pilot in a marina accident (6)
9 Rang the bell again, we hear, like Hawthorne's "Tales" (5–4)
11 Just passing a bun is amusing in an odd way (5)
12 Pretty slice, the last of the pie (4)
13 Legal prohibition where roads meet (10)
15 Seems to be A&P fruit (7)
17 Baby puppies make a mess! (6)
19 Twins, for example, returning to '60s dress fashion (6)
20 With saber pointing west, Ed dozed (7)
22 A wild calf dashes for a one-course meal (5, 5)
23 All right, add a third of a radish to the gumbo (4)
26 Regret about little Everett in the theater presentation (5)
27 Beginning of equation, x = 10 + 100e, in actuality (9)
28 Yale is beaten handily (6)
29 Uninformed, and crazily ranting about nothing (8)

DOWN

1 The dictator has a car, a car redesigned on an early Ford model (8)
2 Poison? Not so! (5)
3 Stagger up and look slyly (4)
4 To predict operating cost in a rough way (13)
6 Sign of vindication after the guillotine (10)
7 Eats amidst cow sounds, causing gloom (9)
8 Examine vinyl on shower hose (6)
10 Deception using 104 cards? (6–7)
14 Is leg-clamp trouble the witch's doing? (5, 5)
16 Jam the wildlife areas (9)
18 Next to a disc jockey, a penny (8)
21 Arise to naturally when a company of sailors gets a hearing (6)
24 Stricken Yankee hiding south of Ethiopia (5)
25 Up to/down to a German king (4)

F I G U R E 39 ▪ *A puzzle entitled "Dirty Jokes" by Henry Hook. Another example of the current trend in American crosswords. Printed by kind permission of Henry Hook.*

ACROSS

1 Butter servings
5 "St. John's Passion" composer
9 Nontalker
13 Investigator of a sort
17 Novelist Ambler
18 Italian bread
19 About ⅓ of Hispaniola
20 ——— Yankees
21 Countertenor
22 Neighbor of Provo
23 Synthetic
24 "J'y suis, j'y ———"
25 Chimney sweeps' kits?
27 The Crudfather et al.?
29 Waif
30 Gloomy tune
32 Δ δ
33 Not used, as a gun
37 Doesn't keep one's distance
39 Goren–Sharif coup
40 Machine for glazing paper
42 Filled (with)
45 Type of 7-digit no.
47 Baton Rouge campus
48 Freedom, à la 1960s
50 "The Blue Eagle"
51 Spanish wine
53 Mid-morning mess?
61 "Lord, is ———?"
62 Goethe's "Der ——— -König"
63 Dilapidated
64 Limp
66 V.I.P.
70 Del ———, Texas
71 Highway section

72 Scholarly
73 Watch, in Chartres
75 Shoe size
76 Bird of myth
77 Constitutional foul-up?
83 Singer Paul and kin
85 Take a powder
86 Chap
87 Turmeric
88 Segar's Olive
89 Crusoe's prototype
93 Corrective
97 Sloop part
99 Snicks' partner
101 "Jumbo" star
102 Hit hard
104 Do to do
106 Study course at Harvard
107 Offensive?
110 Filthy painting?
115 "———— Is Born"
116 Geometry homework, maybe
117 Frost, e.g.
118 "Every inch a king"
119 Pooh's creator
120 Fish stories
121 Something to cop
122 Perry's battlefield
123 Takes in (a movie)
124 Victory: Ger.
125 High-pitched cries
126 Nursery wear: Slang

D O W N

1 TV dinner feature
2 Woody's kid
3 Belgrade name
4 FDR's Fala
5 Inflated
6 Ostentation
7 Nicene, e.g.
8 Surrounds
9 Guatemalan president, 1814–65
10 "———— Marlene"
11 Minuscule part
12 Emulated the Seven Dwarfs
13 Courtroom faction, at times
14 Pollute?
15 Puts in a chip
16 Louis et al.
19 Algerian massif
20 Billy Goats' foe
26 Pedestrian's woe
28 Blue-ribbon word
31 Grid VIP
33 Bruins
34 The elephant and donkey were his
35 Chimney duct
36 Farmer's place
38 Usually between 5 and 6:30 A.M.
41 ". . . the sea-o"
43 Sweetheart, to Sean
44 "———— loaf is . . ."
46 Admit
49 Georgia Tech deg.
51 Pornographic
52 Kind of step or kick
54 Can't do without
55 Circumnavigations
56 7th Ave. merchandise
57 Wojtyla
58 Work allotment
59 "———— the Raven, 'Nevermore' "
60 Cohort of Kent and Lane
65 Kadiddlehopper
66 Vital fluids
67 U. of Maine site
68 Result of Raleigh's gallantry?
69 Steel plow pioneer
71 Thighbone
73 Weasels' kin
74 Scott Joplin rendition
78 End for eye or hand
79 Girlwatched
80 Hibernia
81 Unadulterated
82 One kind is tall
84 Gov. Hammond's constituents
89 Anagram of "nest"
90 Ade's "Fables ————"
91 Playtime or naptime
92 Mauna ————
94 Matadors' capes
95 Part of QED
96 Wasted time
98 NYSE purchase
100 Like Oscar Madison
102 Count at the keyboard
103 Crucial times
105 Town in So. Italy
107 NFL team
108 Opposite of faux
109 "Able was ———— . . ."
111 Vehicle with 4-wheel drive
112 Opposite of domani
113 Minsky's problem
114 No trick-taker, this

■ F I V E ■

The Double-Crostic

As with any art form, it was simply a matter of time before the crossword puzzle engendered a series of spin-offs. The limits of the crossword had become increasingly restrictive by the late 1920's; predictability ruled with the repetition of crossword clichés. Until Mrs. Farrar improved the puzzle in 1942 to suit *New York Times* standards, other routes were explored by dedicated word-game enthusiasts. From these experiments came the Double-Crostic, a hybrid that combined the crossword diagram and the acrostic with the added element of literature.

This direct offspring of the crossword was the handiwork not of a feverish newspaperman but rather of a former schoolteacher, Mrs. Elizabeth Seelman Kingsley. Long a master at the scrambled word pies and brainteasers of the *St. Nicholas* "Riddle-Box" section, Mrs. Kingsley had easily conquered the early crosswords. Even during her first teaching days in Brooklyn, she exhibited a taste for word puzzles by breaking up her lectures with simple guessing games that tested her students on their familiarity with famous fictional characters.

When she was widowed in 1926, a well-intentioned niece sent her a book of puzzles as a small diversion. Although Mrs. Kingsley found the book a welcome distraction, the challenge was minimal. The previous year she had tried her hand at construction, submitting a "good, stiff" crossword to *The Chicago Daily News* for which she received a neat $10. Having proved to herself that she could make as well as solve crosswords, she retired from the pursuit. She recognized a certain thrill in working a puzzle, but it disturbed her that the puzzles seemed to have no real goal.

Since her marriage in 1914, Mrs. Kingsley had devoted herself to the duties expected of the wife of the Massachusetts State Supervisor of Secondary Education. Now, without anyone to keep house for, she turned her mind to career choices and decided to return to work. Rather than return to teaching, she decided to try publishing. She soon got a job as a secretary at Houghton Mifflin in Boston. After a short internship there, she moved on to a position as office manager at the Babson Institute of Business Administration (now Babson College) in the suburb of Babson Park. Apparently the work did not satisfy her, for in the early 1930's she decided to return to her sisters and brother in Brooklyn and start again.

While attending a college reunion at Wellesley, she stumbled across the missing element that would result in the invention of the Double-Crostic. A bit unsettled by the immense popularity of James Joyce and Gertrude Stein among the students, she lamented the lack of attention paid to classical writers. All the attention lavished upon these upstarts deprived her personal favorites (Shakespeare, Defoe and Keats) of their fair share. One way to revive the classics would be to devise a puzzle that would use the works of leading British and American writers; the literary excerpts would keep their works alive while providing a goal for the solver. The crossword grid could be used to contain the letters of the quotation, but she still had to figure out a workable clue structure for such a puzzle.

Using anagram letters (similar to latter-day Scrabble® tiles), Mrs. Kingsley spelled out one of her favorite quotations, then scrambled all the letters. Once they were completely disarranged, she picked out the letters that appeared in the name of the author and work in question. These she laid out vertically in acrostic form. Each of these initial letters was then combined with the remaining letters to form other words; no extraneous letters were used. She then assigned numbers to the letters to indicate where they belonged in the diagram; by transposing the letters to their corresponding boxes, the quotation would emerge. Meanwhile, the author's name and the title of the work would be revealed in the acrostic that accompanied the grid. Within six months, Mrs. Kingsley had produced a hundred puzzles of this type, which she called "double crostic" to represent the dual nature of the game.

After she showed her work to a few friends, someone suggested *The Saturday Review of Literature* as the logical outlet. With a portfolio under her arm, Mrs. Kingsley asked to see someone in authority. Associate editor Amy Loveman talked to her. At first glance, the double crostic certainly appeared suitable for *The Saturday Review*, but it would require further examination by the rest of the staff. The editors studied the puzzles over the weekend; by Tuesday a contract had been drawn up in which Mrs. Kingsley was asked to sell the rights of the name "Double-Crostic" to *The Saturday Review* and to produce a puzzle for each weekly issue.

The maiden puzzle made an impressive début: it was an excerpt from Alfred Lord Tennyson's "Ulysses"—perhaps in an effort to depose Joyce's efforts, which Mrs. Kingsley found greatly overrated (Fig. 40).

Since the diagram so greatly resembled that of the crossword, the workings of the Double-Crostic were carefully explained to the reader. Next to each straightforward Definition stood a row of numbered horizontal dashes designed to accommodate the letters of the answer. After each Word was defined, the individual letters were transposed into the correct box in the grid, which was indicated by number. Once the grid was completed, the quote read from left to right. The author's name and the title were revealed in acrostic fashion by reading the first letters of the definitions vertically. To ensure that the readers were completely clear on the rather elaborate directions, it was specified that "up and down, the letters mean nothing! The black squares indicate ends of words; therefore words do not necessarily end at the right side of the diagram." In conclusion, the editors asked that the readers not be reticent to offer opinions on the Double-Crostic.

Response was enthusiastic as competitive readers around the country sent in letters reporting the record times in which they had conquered the puzzle. In Nebraska, one instant fan astutely analyzed its make-up: "Evolution of old-fashioned square word and numerical acrostic, through modified crossword puzzle." A New Jersey woman, who referred to herself as "The Average Puzzler," claimed to have filled in the acrostic initials after guessing only half a dozen words. A New Yorker found the exclamation point punctuating the sentence explaining the lack of down entries a bit condescending, and thereafter it was eliminated.

Firmly ensconced in her new role, Mrs. Kingsley happily gave up her job hunt and devoted herself to reviving quotations from the old classics that she so cherished. (In a 1953 tribute entitled "Jubilee for Her D-C Majesty," *The Saturday Review* credited her with having "resuscitated more poets and essayists lost through the centuries than all the English I classes in the U.S.A. combined.") From March 31, 1934 until November 29, 1952 she single-handedly constructed every Double-Crostic.

A true devotee of literature and literary efforts, Mrs. Kingsley was a portly woman who, despite her literary preferences, bore a strange resemblance to Gertrude Stein. With a steady income of $10,000 a year to rely upon, she moved into Manhattan, where she took up residence at the Henry Hudson Hotel.

In a short time, she developed quite a following, which included such notables as Arthur Hays Sulzberger (who even tried his hand at Double-Crostic construction), Cole Porter, Cornelia Otis Skinner, Ambassador Joseph Grew and Ogden Nash, who once declared that "Double-Crostics have saved my sanity in the grim loneliness of hotel rooms when I lecture my way around the country." In the opinion of Norman Cousins, "The Double-Crostic is to the crossword puzzle what chess is to checkers. It utilizes the basic form but contains an extra dimension that enables the squares to emerge in a striking quotation." Mrs. Kingsley (also called fondly "Our Queen Elizabeth") thrived on the attention; somehow she seemed to regard the puzzles as surrogate children and their fans as friends of the family. She held court as she worked, planning her puzzles on a black felt square using anagram blocks. Fans soon became friends. She also kept up a hectic correspondence with many of her estimated 10,000 devoted followers. ("I have nests of puzzlers at Yale and other universities," she noted proudly.) Among her distinguished academic admirers were Dr. Edward Delavan Perry, a Columbia University professor of Greek who compulsively tracked the Double-Crostic words to their Greek roots and filed them, and the Dean Emeritus of Engineering at the University of Michigan, Professor Mortimer Cooley, who thanked her for distracting him from his arthritis.

The Crostics Club column that accompanied the "D-C" (as she preferred to call the puzzle) acted as an organ to consolidate Mrs. Kingsley's vast and scattered following. From 1942 until mid-1946, this chatty, rambling feature reported on births, deaths and additions to the general D-C fraternity (Fig. 41). Fans in isolated enclaves who wrote inquiring if any fellow D-Cers lived in neighboring areas would receive prompt satisfaction. "Of the many kicks I get out of doing this column, not the least is the knowledge that it seems to act as a clearing-house of personalities," she exulted.

The column also afforded readers an opportunity to make suggestions and to send in corrections. In this way, an informal forum developed in which the use of obscure words was debated. One memorable furor arose in the early forties over the use of the slangy word "tow-row" (*Webster's New International Dictionary: colloq.* rumpus). Much to Mrs. Kingsley's relief, a lady in Massachusetts came to her rescue by citing the use of this

Directions: To solve this puzzle, you must guess twenty-five words, the definitions of which are given in the column headed *Definitions*. The letters in each word to be guessed are numbered (these numbers appear at the beginning of each definition) and you are thereby able to tell how many letters are in the required word. When you have guessed a word each letter is to be written in the correspondingly numbered square on the puzzle diagram. When the squares are all filled in you will find (by reading from left to right) a quotation from a famous author. Reading up and down, the letters mean nothing! The black squares indicate ends of words; therefore words do not necessarily end at the right side of the diagram.

Either before (preferably) or after placing the letters in their squares you should write the Words you have guessed on the blank lines which appear to the right in the column headed *Words*. The initial letters of this list of words spell the name of the author and the title of the piece from which the quotation has been taken.

DEFINITIONS	WORDS
I. 1–14–23–50–95. A perfume of roses.	I. _____
II. 145–6–28–90–137. Child's game played with cards and numbers.	II. _____
III. 97–8–79–146–98–61–75–77–76–32–27–19–133. Light as a feather.	III. _____
IV. 80–85–60–113–51–58–48. Held in high esteem; worshipped.	IV. _____
V. 81–172–31–84–24–176–65–89. Insubstantial.	V. _____
VI. 112–45–114–164–149–173–142–36. The business section of a city.	VI. _____
VII. 144–102–2–63. Material for bandages.	VII. _____
VIII. 37–4–66–82–110–116–62. Upholstered backless seat.	VIII. _____
IX. 100–106–33–5–122–41–138–69–83–13–162–127. A Russian pianist.	IX. _____
X. 40–59–52–25. A drupe with a single seed.	X. _____
XI. 135–175–3–73. Movement of the ocean.	XI. _____
XII. 130–43–129–107–111–55–139–47. To alienate.	XII. _____
XIII. 15–121–92–136–101–39. A mighty hunter.	XIII. _____
XIV. 167–9–140–46–105. Artless; simple.	XIV. _____
XV. 119–54–104–17–153–34. Hebrew God.	XV. _____
XVI. 134–64–128–168–16–30. Flat, dark image.	XVI. _____
XVII. 155–125–78–148–143–165–158–56. Prejudiced (compound).	XVII. _____
XVIII. 12–96–120–11–7–170–150–21–68–174. Significant, unusual.	XVIII. _____
XIX. 87–141–171–161–67–20–10–126. Not propitious.	XIX. _____
XX. 177–99–152–163–108–115. Member of the tribe of Levi.	XX. _____

Clues to Figure 40 continue on page 148.

XXI. 42–88–26–159–49–91. Doodle dandy.   XXI. _____

XXII. 22–71–151–118–131–147–38–94–160–29. Watchword (Bibl.).   XXII. _____

XXIII. 109–86–132–124–72–117–123–178. Uttered a harsh sound.   XXIII. _____

XXIV. 157–44–93–53–166–18–35–103. Forceful.   XXIV. _____

XXV. 156–154–74–169–70–57. To stop the flow.   XXV. _____

word in Robert Louis Stevenson's classic *Kidnapped*, therefore making its use acceptable. Another controversy resulted when she gave a quote by Kenneth Roberts in which Maine chowder was compared with French bouillabaisse—to the detriment of the latter. The publicity from this conflict won Mr. Roberts a commission to write the introduction to a cookbook of Maine specialities.

Always willing to admit mistakes ("Such erudition justifies my contention that my puzzlers are far wiser than am I," she humbly wrote upon being chastised), she thanked readers for keeping her on her toes. Some followers even accused her of slipping in a crossword cliché on occasion. Mrs. Kingsley exonerated herself by confessing that her work was so all-consuming that it prevented her from ever examining the state of crosswords to check for such overlaps. "But it would be most natural for both of us when confronted with an impasse to find an easy way out with a much-used word," she explained, adding that there was "nothing reprehensible" in this coincidence.

She welcomed audience participation, especially where her Crostics books for Simon and Schuster were concerned. This series first appeared several months after her *Saturday Review* début in 1934. With the overwhelming popularity of the crossword series well established, the publishers immediately offered Mrs. Kingsley a contract to create a similar collection of Double-Crostics. In the foreword to the fiftieth Crostics collection, Simon and Schuster admitted that although they would have loved to take credit for the popularization of the Double-Crostic as well as for the crossword, "the fact is that in this case all we did was adopt the baby."

By January of 1946, Mrs. Kingsley was at work on Series #20. At that time, she took the opportunity to discuss the curious case of one of her entries for this particular book. Her work on the series often provided material for the *Saturday Review* column. Carelessly, she had misplaced one D-C; recalling the quotation, she started from scratch. This second effort appeared in the book. When she came across the "lost" puzzle, she compared it with the one that had been published. As she had always suspected, the two were completely different—proving her theory that if she had more time to tamper with the puzzles she could come up with an alternate scheme for each one.

During World War II, the Crostics Club included notes on D-Cers in the service. Mrs. Kingsley was most concerned that this dedicated branch of fans keep in touch. One young corporal on Okinawa complained that the unreliable mail service made it frustrating to work a D-C, since solutions

1 I	2 E	3 V		4 G	5 B	6 P	7 M	8 H	9 A	10 W	11 X
12 N		13 D	14 H	15 X	16 E		17 N	18 L		19 O	20 F	21 M	22 H	23 K	24 R	25 N
26 A	27 T	28 J		29 B	30 K	31 G	32 N	33 Y	34 M	35 Q		36 P	37 B	38 K	39 F
40 Y	41 D		42 V		43 G	44 N	45 H	46 A	47 B	48 X	49 C	50 P	51 F	52 R	53 C
54 I	55 B		56 Q	57 L	58 V	59 S		60 O	61 W	62 H	63 K	64 B	65 A	66 Q	67 S
68 K	69 V		70 W	71 F	72 K	73 G	74 B	75 A	76 X	77 L		78 K	79 V	80 C	81 L
82 D	83 I	84 L	85 Y		86 L	87 S	88 R	89 E	90 F		91 E	92 J	93 A		94 C	95 B
96 W	97 X	98 E	99 K	100 U		101 U	102 K	103 J		104 N	105 Q	106 C		107 J	108 M	109 W
110 S	111 K	112 E	113 U	114 R		115 P	116 T	117 C	118 H	119 Y	120 L		121 J	122 Y		123 H
124 N	125 T		126 Q	127 V		128 P	129 U	130 A	131 I	132 V		133 B	134 D	135 M	136 P
137 Q	138 C	139 Y	140 A		141 C		142 O	143 R	144 S	145 X	146 T	147 B	148 P	149 V		150 D
151 A	152 L	153 E		154 C	155 I		156 A		157 T	158 P	159 M	160 B	161 Y	162 U	163 R	164 H
	165 F	166 T		167 E	168 A	169 F		170 G	171 X	172 I	173 V		174 P	175 X	176 B	177 F
178 D	179 O		180 J	181 N		182 O	183 N	184 U	185 W	186 Y						

D E F I N I T I O N S

W O R D S

A. Fabulous lean medieval monster who fed on patient wives.

 __75__ __168__ __26__ __46__ __140__ __93__ __65__ __156__ __9__ __151__ __130__

B. Novel by Edith Wharton (1905) (with *The*).

 __95__ __64__ __160__ __29__ __37__ __147__ __55__ __5__ __74__ __47__ __176__ __133__

C. Celebrating victory as applied to an ode.

 __106__ __49__ __154__ __117__ __138__ __94__ __80__ __141__ __53__

D. Flat, wide river valley often used with name of river.

 __41__ __150__ __178__ __134__ __82__ __13__

E. The black varnish tree or the varnish.

 __167__ __2__ __16__ __89__ __91__ __153__ __98__ __112__

F. Introductory part of a discourse.

 __169__ __20__ __165__ __90__ __39__ __51__ __177__ __71__

G. Appraised: assessed for value.

$\overline{73}$ $\overline{4}$ $\overline{170}$ $\overline{31}$ $\overline{43}$

H. Monk of a reformed Cistercian order (U.S. 1848).

$\overline{118}$ $\overline{22}$ $\overline{14}$ $\overline{62}$ $\overline{123}$ $\overline{8}$ $\overline{45}$ $\overline{164}$

I. Eccentric.

$\overline{54}$ $\overline{172}$ $\overline{1}$ $\overline{131}$ $\overline{155}$ $\overline{83}$

J. One of the Vanir (Norse myth).

$\overline{28}$ $\overline{107}$ $\overline{180}$ $\overline{103}$ $\overline{121}$ $\overline{92}$

K. Mere apprehension of an object.

$\overline{38}$ $\overline{30}$ $\overline{102}$ $\overline{63}$ $\overline{72}$ $\overline{111}$ $\overline{23}$ $\overline{78}$ $\overline{99}$

L. Fruitless and endless (Gr. myth).

$\overline{120}$ $\overline{68}$ $\overline{77}$ $\overline{86}$ $\overline{152}$ $\overline{81}$ $\overline{57}$ $\overline{84}$ $\overline{18}$

M. Beguile; to ensnare.

$\overline{34}$ $\overline{159}$ $\overline{135}$ $\overline{7}$ $\overline{108}$ $\overline{21}$

N. Epithet applied to Andrea del Sarto as a painter (see Browning's poem).

$\overline{181}$ $\overline{17}$ $\overline{124}$ $\overline{32}$ $\overline{104}$ $\overline{183}$ $\overline{44}$ $\overline{12}$ $\overline{25}$

O. Alleviates.

$\overline{19}$ $\overline{60}$ $\overline{142}$ $\overline{179}$ $\overline{182}$

P. Applied to the tract of unsettled Territory not in 13 Colonies in 1776.

$\overline{174}$ $\overline{158}$ $\overline{148}$ $\overline{128}$ $\overline{36}$ $\overline{115}$ $\overline{6}$ $\overline{136}$ $\overline{50}$

Q. What Peter Schlemihl surrendered to the devil.

$\overline{56}$ $\overline{105}$ $\overline{66}$ $\overline{35}$ $\overline{126}$ $\overline{137}$

R. Spirit that actuates moral attitudes in a people.

$\overline{114}$ $\overline{88}$ $\overline{143}$ $\overline{163}$ $\overline{52}$ $\overline{24}$

S. Carrion: garbage.

$\overline{144}$ $\overline{59}$ $\overline{87}$ $\overline{110}$ $\overline{67}$

T. To get to the bottom of.

$\overline{166}$ $\overline{116}$ $\overline{125}$ $\overline{146}$ $\overline{27}$ $\overline{157}$

U. Indian of whose people Tecumseh was Chief.

$\overline{113}$ $\overline{129}$ $\overline{184}$ $\overline{101}$ $\overline{149}$ $\overline{162}$ $\overline{100}$

V. Applied to the Hydra Hercules killed (2nd Labor).

$\overline{58}$ $\overline{3}$ $\overline{132}$ $\overline{127}$ $\overline{42}$ $\overline{173}$ $\overline{79}$ $\overline{69}$

W. A *Way* most famous of Roman roads.

$\overline{70}$ $\overline{61}$ $\overline{109}$ $\overline{96}$ $\overline{10}$ $\overline{185}$

X. Oblivion to external reality: final emancipation (Hinduism).

$\overline{11}$ $\overline{48}$ $\overline{171}$ $\overline{15}$ $\overline{175}$ $\overline{97}$ $\overline{76}$

Y. Fiber of a tropical hedge used in making paper and cord.

$\overline{186}$ $\overline{40}$ $\overline{161}$ $\overline{145}$ $\overline{33}$ $\overline{122}$ $\overline{139}$ $\overline{85}$ $\overline{119}$

might not be forthcoming. In addition, the absence of reference books increased the challenge, sometimes almost unbearably. "We have in the battery a considerable number of regular crossword fans and when crosswords aren't available, they come and try to help on your D-C's . . . I hope you can see that a D-Cer's life on Okinawa is not an easy one," he wrote.

The column was discontinued in the summer of 1946 in the interests of space and better presentation of the Double-Crostic itself. Many readers had been complaining of the cramped manner in which the D-C was published; because of the column, it was squeezed into a small portion of the page. In order to present the D-C properly and with the dignity it deserved, the column was sacrificed. In her Christmas letter of December 7 that year, Mrs. Kingsley thanked those sympathetic readers who missed the column—which was "lost deliberately," she noted, a bit accusingly, "at your request." She then gracefully picked up where she had left off a year earlier by updating her followers on changes within the fraternity as well as including a few *mea culpa*s where she felt they applied. She ended the letter with a New Year's wish that she might continue this seasonal type of message "space permitting." Apparently this wish was granted, as the Christmas letter continued to appear through 1950.

During her lifetime, Mrs. Kingsley produced some 2,500 Double-Crostics, 975 for *The Saturday Review*, twenty-six volumes for Simon and Schuster, plus a fortnightly puzzle for *The New York Times* Sunday magazine instituted at the insistence of its great fan, publisher Sulzberger. The puzzle retained its name, The Kingsley Double-Crostic, in *The Times*, with credit given to *The Saturday Review*, owner of the D-C trademark. (Will Weng later revised this policy by changing the name of the puzzle. The D-C had already appeared in other publications under a variety of pseudonyms and there was no reason now not to follow suit, thereby eliminating *The Saturday Review* by-line. *The New York Time*'s puzzle, which had become a monthly feature, then became known as The Acrostic Puzzle, a name it still carries today.)

Mrs. Kingsley also received several free-lance commissions. In 1938 *Banking Magazine* requested six puzzles based on quotations dealing with financial topics. For one of these custom-made puzzles, she used the Benjamin Franklin quote, "All men are not equally qualified for getting money." *Harper's Bazaar* ordered a fashion puzzle in 1951, which she managed to fit in between other commitments. Occasionally, Mrs. Kingsley wrote D-C's for private customers; the most prominent recipient of such a puzzle was Edsel Ford. For three years one of his friends, knowing his enthusiasm for puzzles, ordered special Double-Crostics in honor of the auto manufacturer's birthday. The friend requested that these D-C's be based on quotations from an obscure Scottish poet. However, Mrs. Kingsley found these excerpts "gloomy and horrible" and abandoned this unsuitable material for "some simple classical notes."

Surrounded by her constant companions—reference books such as *Webster's New International Dictionary*, *A Dictionary of Synonyms*, *The American Thesaurus of Slang*, Edith Hamilton's *Mythology*—Mrs. Kingsley was never at a loss for work. For extra help, she relied on her membership to the Mercantile Library on East 47th Street in New York City. Except for an occasional foray to that library, her life seems to have been rather sedentary. She did venture back to Brooklyn to visit her siblings on occasion; she also enjoyed attending concerts at Carnegie Hall from time to time.

In the summers, she devoted herself to the pursuit of worthwhile quotes with which to fill her Double-Crostics. This meant traveling to various libraries and colleges that housed original materials. Series #23, for example, focused on American letters. While researching this topic, she discovered that her favorite authors were James Madison and John Jay—much to her chagrin, as the letter "J" presented a stumbling block in the construction of clues.

"Contrary to crosswords, the use of words is just a means to an end—the quotation," she reminded her fans. Often in the line of duty she was forced to do extensive detective work. The words "gung ho" required such an effort. Mrs. Kingsley consulted several knowledgeable librarians at the New York Public Library before Dr. Mitchell of the Oriental Department confirmed that it was a Chinese term that meant "working together." During the war, the phrase had become a slogan for Carlson's Raiders, and from there crept into the language as a colloquialism.

Reference books were—and are—a mainstay to the D-C fan. Without them, Mrs. Kingsley would have never been able to build her impressive D-C empire. Memory accounted for only a small part of the process. Once a former classmate of hers, one-time Congresswoman Ruth Baker Pratt, asked her: "Elizabeth, quickly, who built the Trojan horse?" Without pausing to reflect, Mrs. Kingsley simply replied, "Frankly, I do not know." Her achievement lay in her ability to craft a workable Double-Crostic and not in her extensive store of knowledge. In his book on crosswords, the British constructor Ximenes noted that the average solver demands that the vocabulary contained within a puzzle conform to that of the man in the street. But the more elitist group of devoted solvers allow for the use of reference books when it is called for, as in the case of the D-C (Fig. 42).

Despite the great appreciation exhibited by her admirers, Mrs. Kingsley felt that few people understood the intellectual discipline required by her occupation. She set very high standards for herself in the construction of her Double-Crostics, as the erudite quality of her clues made clear. She never let a useful word slip away but always jotted down odd terms in a small brown notebook that never left her side. To one of her correspondents she wrote: "Many complain of my use of mythological terms. Do you realize that 'H's' are the bane of my existence, being as common as they are, and that 'H's' predominate in Greek, Hebrew, Hindu, and other Oriental words?" Defensively, she added: "If you were constructing a puzzle and had letters left over and they made a Vedic deity, what would you do?"

As Mrs. Kingsley grew older, she found it increasingly difficult to keep up D-C production. (Mrs. Farrar reported that, in later years, Mrs. Kingsley could speak of nothing else but her involvement with the puzzle.) She retired in 1952 at the age of seventy-four and her editor, Doris Nash Wortman, took over. A former president of the National Puzzlers' League, Mrs. Wortman had been a proficient constructor ever since the late 1930's, when she sent a Double-Crostic written as a valentine to her husband, Elbert, to Mrs. Kingsley's fan section. Since 1944 she had been proofreading *The Saturday Review* D-C's, having begun her career with the Crostic Series #10 in 1938–39. But when her first puzzle appeared on December 6, 1952, she was relatively unknown.

The transition was made as inconspicuously as possible: the title "Kingsley Double-Crostic" reassured readers that the tradition would be carried on with the same grace as before (Fig. 43).

Mrs. Wortman was known to be an extraordinarily good-natured woman. Through her years of collaboration with Mrs. Kingsley, she had only kind words for her mentor. "All in all, it was a pleasant union of Smith and Wellesley," she once remarked (having graduated from Smith College in 1911). Mrs. Wortman's work reflects this light-hearted strain, distinguishing it from Mrs. Kingsley's more scholarly turn of mind. For "hatch" she once used the humorous clue: "Out for the chick, up for the plotter, down for the sailor." She began to use more contemporary quotations and sometimes opted for a fanciful phrase or word of her own invention: a blatant violation of all crossword-puzzle rules, which tacitly stipulate that the answer must be familiar. For example, she used the clue "The corn is evidently higher than Hammerstein thought" for the answer "giraffe's eye." Of course, such an occasional transgression did not interfere with the rest of the puzzle but clearly drew the line between the two Double-Crostic regimes.

Mrs. Wortman's columns were also punctuated by more verve than those of her predecessor. But in her work habits, she was every bit as sober as Mrs. Kingsley. Her daughter revealed that she worked steadily from the time she arose at about five A.M. until bedtime at eleven.

Unknown to her fans, Mrs. Wortman's happy-go-lucky demeanor hid an unhappy home life. Apparently, Mr. Wortman was not as successful as his wife; his business deals always seemed to fall through, leaving Mrs. Wortman to contend with financial crises. Fortunately, her $15,000 salary kept the family afloat while Mr. Wortman moved from job to job. Perhaps it was this situation that motivated her to immerse herself so deeply in her work; and perhaps it was also the reason for her growing carelessness in construction and definition.

During the mid-sixties intent solvers began to notice a loss of integrity in the D-C. Among the more indignant fans was novelist Laura Z. Hobson (*Gentleman's Agreement*), who, while working a Double-Crostic, came across a definition that elicited an unexpectedly offensive answer, especially to the eye of one as sensitive to bias as Hobson. The definition "Describing some of the people in the South" was answered by "Blacks and tans." As a shocked Laura Hobson began to scrutinize future puzzles more carefully, she uncovered similar lapses as well as grammatical errors.

When she could no longer endure these transgressions, Hobson appealed to her friend Norman Cousins, the publisher of *Saturday Review*. When she told him of the strange things that had been happening to the D-C, he asked her to become Double-Crostic editor. In this capacity she watched over Mrs. Wortman's shoulder. Using her newly found powers, she killed two D-C's that she considered unsuitable for the magazine. The first contained an antilabor quote, while the second was excerpted from a John Masefield poem on the assassination of John F. Kennedy. The escapist aspects of puzzle-solving did not seem to be aptly represented by these choices, and the editor was not about to allow them to appear in print.

Upon Mrs. Wortman's death in 1967, her husband offered his services to *The Saturday Review*. When his offer was declined, he called the magazine's offices to say that it was he who had masterminded the Double-

FIGURE 42 ▪ *This Double-Crostic by Elizabeth S. Kingsley from* The Saturday Review, *October 30, 1943, was accompanied by a short account of the party given by the magazine at the Coffee House Club in New York to commemorate the "birth" of the 500th D-C. "As I had been forewarned only of the time and place and the distinguished quality of the guests, I was really terrified at the prospect of meeting such a concentrated group," Mrs. Kingsley wrote modestly. "But they were as chatty and unassuming as are the SRL associates," she added. Reprinted from* The Saturday Review, *1290 Avenue of the Americas, New York, N.Y. 10019. Copyright © 1943 by* The Saturday Review.

						1 X	2 F		3 M	4 B	5 E	6 R	7 D	
8 T	9 Q	10 G	11 H	12 F	13 W	14 E		15 P	16 N	17 S		18 W	19 F	20 C	21 V	22 H
23 I	24 Q		25 C	26 P	27 O		28 W	29 I	30 L		31 N	32 E	33 F		34 R	35 E
36 C		37 W	38 B	39 T	40 O	41 R	42 X	43 D		44 A	45 R		46 N	47 T	48 D	49 M
50 X	51 J	52 R	53 B	54 S	55 L		56 O	57 N		58 I	59 C	60 G		61 X	62 M	63 Y
64 S	65 C		66 H	67 O	68 K	69 A		70 E	71 L	72 C	73 O		74 X	75 W	76 N	77 J
78 D	79 Q	80 Y	81 T		82 Y	83 L	84 H	85 I	86 T	87 V	88 F	89 X	90 J	91 K		92 E
93 K	94 G		95 P	96 I	97 R		98 H	99 K	100 L	101 J	102 X	103 G	104 I	105 C	106 E
107 P	108 S	109 E		110 L	111 D	112 I	113 H	114 S	115 F	116 N	117 Q	118 E		119 M	120 E	121 N
122 F		123 P	124 W	125 I	126 R	127 D	128 S	129 G	130 X	131 N	132 Q		133 P	134 G		135 S
136 D	137 L	138 R	139 M		140 N	141 P		142 O	143 Y	144 K	145 S	146 L	147 A	148 N	149 I	150 P
	151 R	152 P		153 P	154 E	155 O		156 U	157 G	158 B	159 S	160 Y		161 V	162 Y	163 Q
164 I	165 F	166 K		167 O	168 P	169 E		170 S	171 N	172 P		173 Q	174 H	175 X	176 U	177 Y
178 W	179 R	180 L		181 C	182 X	183 M	184 F	185 U							

DEFINITIONS

WORDS

A. Modified and amplified form of Esperanto (1907).

— — —
147 69 44

B. National leader of India.

— — — — —
53 158 66 4 38

C. Plant used by Michael to purge Adam's eyes (Milton).

— — — — — — — —
36 105 181 59 65 72 20 25

D. Replete with gusto, relish, piquancy.

— — — — — — —
78 111 7 43 127 136 48

E. To remain before the public (3 wds.).

— — — — — — — — — — —
35 5 118 109 70 92 14 32 120 154 106 169

F. Mirthless.

— — — — — — — — —
115 19 33 122 165 88 12 184 2

G. Those who peel pulpwood logs (logging).

$\overline{103}\ \overline{157}\ \overline{134}\ \overline{94}\ \overline{60}\ \overline{129}\ \overline{10}$

H. French painter of shepherdesses, etc. (1684–1721).

$\overline{98}\ \overline{22}\ \overline{84}\ \overline{11}\ \overline{76}\ \overline{174}\ \overline{113}$

I. Agitated; nervously confused (3 wds.).

$\overline{164}\ \overline{23}\ \overline{112}\ \overline{104}\ \overline{125}\ \overline{149}\ \overline{58}\ \overline{96}\ \overline{29}\ \overline{85}$

J. Is for the moment inattentive.

$\overline{77}\ \overline{51}\ \overline{101}\ \overline{90}$

K. Every one; none being excepted (3 wds.).

$\overline{166}\ \overline{99}\ \overline{144}\ \overline{91}\ \overline{93}\ \overline{68}$

L. Descendants of first settlers of French origin in Canada.

$\overline{71}\ \overline{55}\ \overline{110}\ \overline{137}\ \overline{30}\ \overline{83}\ \overline{100}\ \overline{146}\ \overline{180}$

M. Novel by George Meredith (with *The*).

$\overline{139}\ \overline{3}\ \overline{183}\ \overline{49}\ \overline{119}\ \overline{62}$

N. Mixture of finely cut vegetables in soup or salad dressing.

$\overline{46}\ \overline{16}\ \overline{131}\ \overline{116}\ \overline{148}\ \overline{31}\ \overline{57}\ \overline{140}\ \overline{121}\ \overline{171}$

O. A skylight (Fr.).

$\overline{167}\ \overline{142}\ \overline{67}\ \overline{73}\ \overline{40}\ \overline{56}\ \overline{27}\ \overline{155}$

P. Having straight hair (Indians, etc.).

$\overline{150}\ \overline{133}\ \overline{152}\ \overline{141}\ \overline{26}\ \overline{15}\ \overline{172}\ \overline{95}\ \overline{123}\ \overline{153}\ \overline{107}\ \overline{168}$

Q. The ancestor of mankind; father of Prometheus.

$\overline{79}\ \overline{132}\ \overline{173}\ \overline{9}\ \overline{24}\ \overline{117}\ \overline{163}$

R. Unalloyed quality; purest lustre (3 wds.).

$\overline{45}\ \overline{126}\ \overline{179}\ \overline{97}\ \overline{34}\ \overline{6}\ \overline{151}\ \overline{138}\ \overline{41}\ \overline{52}$

S. Clandestinely; secretly (slang: 3 wds.).

$\overline{128}\ \overline{108}\ \overline{159}\ \overline{170}\ \overline{64}\ \overline{135}\ \overline{145}\ \overline{54}\ \overline{17}\ \overline{114}$

T. Virulent.

$\overline{8}\ \overline{47}\ \overline{39}\ \overline{86}\ \overline{81}$

U. Short for Russia's program in May 1921.

$\overline{176}\ \overline{185}\ \overline{156}$

V. Japanese statesman (1841–1909).

$\overline{161}\ \overline{21}\ \overline{87}$

W. The Greeks against Troy (Homer).

$\overline{124}\ \overline{75}\ \overline{28}\ \overline{18}\ \overline{13}\ \overline{178}\ \overline{37}$

X. High and narrow chest of drawers.

$\overline{42}\ \overline{1}\ \overline{175}\ \overline{74}\ \overline{50}\ \overline{61}\ \overline{130}\ \overline{89}\ \overline{102}\ \overline{182}$

Y. Last Anglo-Norman King of England (1135–54).

$\overline{160}\ \overline{177}\ \overline{80}\ \overline{82}\ \overline{63}\ \overline{143}\ \overline{162}$

F I G U R E 43 ▪ *Example of a Kingsley Double-Crostic by Doris Nash Wortman,* from The Saturday Review, *December 6, 1952. Reprinted from* The Saturday Review, *1290 Avenue of the Americas, New York, N.Y. 10019. Copyright © 1952 by* The Saturday Review.

1 A	2 K	▪	3 N	4 W	▪	5 Z'	▪	6 F	7 K	8 T	9 S	10 X	▪	11 G	
12 A	13 U	14 B	▪	15 H	16 Z'	17 D	▪	18 J	▪	19 P	20 E	21 X	22 N	▪	23 B	24 M
25 Y	26 T	27 A	28 D	29 S	30 K	▪	31 W	32 Q	33 Z'	▪	34 J	35 K	▪	36 N	37 A	38 Z'
39 I	40 Z	41 V	42 R	▪	43 D	▪	44 C	45 X	46 F	47 V	▪	48 E	49 L	50 K	51 X	52 Z'
▪	53 N	54 Z	55 J	▪	56 K	57 X	58 Q	▪	59 F	60 U	61 W	62 B	63 H	▪	64 P	65 F
66 V	▪	67 D	68 L	69 X	70 F	71 M	72 K	73 O	74 R	▪	75 O	76 S	77 E	▪	78 W	79 V
80 K	81 S	▪	82 M	83 H	▪	84 K	85 L	86 O	87 Z	88 G	▪	89 Z'	90 I	▪	91 Z	92 A
▪	93 E	94 B	▪	95 B	96 M	97 K	98 C	▪	99 M	100 F	101 Y	▪	102 K	103 P	104 T
105 O	106 U	107 P	▪	108 G	109 M	110 Z'	111 O	112 Y	▪	113 C	114 T	115 O	▪	116 Q	117 Z	118 A
119 Y	▪	120 K	121 V	122 M	▪	123 L	124 T	125 M	▪	126 D	127 S	▪	128 S	129 X	130 Z	131 E
132 N	133 F	134 G	135 J	136 M	137 S	138 I	▪	139 Q	140 G	▪	141 G	142 B	▪	143 Y	144 F	145 P
▪	146 W	147 B	148 A	149 Z	▪	150 J	151 I	152 N	153 B	▪	154 Y	155 T	156 M	157 S	158 U	159 V
160 A	161 H	▪	162 H	163 L	164 X	165 I	▪	166 Z	167 R	168 H	▪	169 U	170 R	171 M	172 O
173 C	174 O	175 Q	176 D	177 L	▪	178 C	179 R	180 U	▪	181 G	182 Z	183 T	184 W		

D E F I N I T I O N S

W O R D S

A. With "Below Stairs," a comedy of 1759 by Rev. James Townley (2 wds.).

<u>1</u> <u>12</u> <u>160</u> <u>37</u> <u>148</u> <u>27</u> <u>92</u> <u>118</u>

B. Son and successor of Count Manuel, in Poictesme novels by Cabell.

<u>142</u> <u>95</u> <u>153</u> <u>94</u> <u>62</u> <u>147</u> <u>23</u> <u>14</u>

C. Any of several forms of a skin disease common to man and domestic animals.

<u>44</u> <u>178</u> <u>173</u> <u>113</u> <u>98</u>

D. See Word J.

<u>43</u> <u>67</u> <u>176</u> <u>126</u> <u>28</u> <u>17</u>

E. Asiatic statesman whose given name contains four a's.

<u>48</u> <u>131</u> <u>93</u> <u>77</u> <u>20</u>

F. Low-cut sports shoes with laces tied around the ankles.

<u>6</u> <u>144</u> <u>100</u> <u>133</u> <u>59</u> <u>65</u> <u>70</u> <u>46</u>

G. Nationalist political party in Egypt.

$\overline{141}\ \overline{181}\ \overline{11}\ \overline{88}\ \overline{134}\ \overline{140}\ \overline{108}$

H. Greek name for their ancient civic goddess, wise in both peace and war.

$\overline{15}\ \overline{162}\ \overline{161}\ \overline{168}\ \overline{63}\ \overline{83}$

I. What Shakespeare said cannot live with crabbed age.

$\overline{165}\ \overline{90}\ \overline{39}\ \overline{138}\ \overline{151}$

J. Followed by Words N and D, Britain, as affectionately described by Thos. Dibdin.

$\overline{150}\ \overline{18}\ \overline{135}\ \overline{34}\ \overline{55}$

K. City in Maryland near mouth of Susquehanna River, famous for its race track.

$\overline{56}\ \overline{120}\ \overline{50}\ \overline{7}\ \overline{30}\ \overline{97}\ \overline{35}\ \overline{72}\ \overline{102}\ \overline{80}\ \overline{84}\ \overline{2}$

L. A classic of Eastern travel, 1844.

$\overline{49}\ \overline{85}\ \overline{68}\ \overline{163}\ \overline{177}\ \overline{123}$

M. Where Dickens' domestic insect lived (3 wds.).

$\overline{24}\ \overline{71}\ \overline{125}\ \overline{82}\ \overline{136}\ \overline{109}\ \overline{122}\ \overline{96}\ \overline{171}\ \overline{156}\ \overline{99}$

N. See Word J.

$\overline{53}\ \overline{3}\ \overline{22}\ \overline{36}\ \overline{132}\ \overline{152}$

O. Trademark for a popular French apéritif.

$\overline{115}\ \overline{86}\ \overline{105}\ \overline{174}\ \overline{111}\ \overline{75}\ \overline{172}\ \overline{73}$

P. Embouchure of a flute, etc.

$\overline{19}\ \overline{145}\ \overline{103}\ \overline{107}\ \overline{64}$

Q. Space surrounding a house, castle, etc.

$\overline{139}\ \overline{58}\ \overline{175}\ \overline{32}\ \overline{116}$

R. Boreal.

$\overline{179}\ \overline{170}\ \overline{167}\ \overline{42}\ \overline{74}$

S. Kansas town famous as stopping place of caravans in Gold Rush.

$\overline{9}\ \overline{81}\ \overline{29}\ \overline{157}\ \overline{128}\ \overline{127}\ \overline{76}\ \overline{137}$

T. Old English publishers of sacred music.

$\overline{104}\ \overline{114}\ \overline{26}\ \overline{8}\ \overline{183}\ \overline{155}\ \overline{124}$

U. Bushy.

$\overline{180}\ \overline{106}\ \overline{169}\ \overline{158}\ \overline{13}\ \overline{60}$

V. Browning's bird that sings his song twice over.

$\overline{47}\ \overline{41}\ \overline{121}\ \overline{159}\ \overline{66}\ \overline{79}$

Clues to Figure 43 continue on page 160. **159**

W. Dean of Columbia College, 1918–43.

$\overline{31}$ $\overline{61}$ $\overline{78}$ $\overline{146}$ $\overline{184}$ $\overline{4}$

X. Greedy.

$\overline{51}$ $\overline{21}$ $\overline{45}$ $\overline{69}$ $\overline{57}$ $\overline{164}$ $\overline{129}$ $\overline{10}$

Y. Ostentatiously stylish.

$\overline{101}$ $\overline{143}$ $\overline{154}$ $\overline{25}$ $\overline{112}$ $\overline{119}$

Z. The black one in pool (2 wds.).

$\overline{54}$ $\overline{91}$ $\overline{40}$ $\overline{117}$ $\overline{130}$ $\overline{182}$ $\overline{166}$ $\overline{149}$ $\overline{87}$

Z^1. A fish which ascends rivers to spawn, as the salmon, etc.

$\overline{5}$ $\overline{16}$ $\overline{110}$ $\overline{89}$ $\overline{52}$ $\overline{38}$ $\overline{33}$

Crostic all these years. (If he had known of Hobson's unfavorable opinion, he might not have been so hasty to make this claim.) Although his overtures were rejected, he insisted briefly and then dropped out of sight.

Several candidates were interviewed for the position of *Saturday Review* Double-Crostic master. After careful consideration, Hobson chose Thomas H. Middleton (coincidentally Norman Cousins's brother-in-law). An actor with several national commercials to his credit, Middleton gracefully took over where his predecessors had left off. With his puzzles the quality of the Double-Crostic improved markedly, according to critics Hobson and Farrar.

Although fans are no longer united by the Crostics Club Column, the fraternity continues to pursue its consuming interest in an informal manner. According to Middleton, fans are forever trying to heighten the challenge with various tales of bravado. The most daring solvers refuse to use reference books at all—quite a challenge even to a well-versed reader. These fanatics chide Middleton when he includes chapter and verse on the Biblical quotes in his clues. The gracious constructor points out that they need not use this tip if they prefer to rely on memory. Others who enjoy tempting fate use a pen, thereby risking the crossword-solver's dilemma of writing over an incorrect entry and blurring the entire diagram. This strategy eliminates the fun of working backwards by filling in some of the grid, deducing the possibilities, and then transferring the presumed letters in the grid back to the words list.

One woman reportedly called *The New York Times* with an unusual query. For years she had been working the Acrostic Puzzle by directly placing the answer in the grid rather than filling in the "words." What were those horizontal spaces meant for, she finally wanted to know. Perhaps Thomas Middleton has a point when he ventures the proposition that "one of the things that sets puzzleheads off from the saner members of society is that we do enjoy making things tougher for ourselves" (Fig. 44).

F I G U R E 44 ▪ *Example of a Kingsley Double-Crostic by Thomas H. Middleton, from* The Saturday Review, *February 16, 1980. Reprinted from* The Saturday Review, *1290 Avenue of the Americas, New York, N.Y. 10019. Copyright © 1980 by* The Saturday Review.

1 S	2 V	3 N	4 C	5 K	■	6 Z	7 F	8 X	■	9 T	10 E	11 I	12 Q	13 O	14 N
15 T	■	16 V	17 C	■	18 A	19 U	20 O	■	21 M	22 T	23 H	24 V	25 P	26 N	27 D	28 R
■	29 V	30 C	31 G	32 X	33 E	34 R	35 O	36 K	37 Y	■	38 D	39 S	40 A	41 O	■	42 J
43 T	■	44 K	45 D	46 W	47 G	■	48 I	49 S	50 L	51 H	■	52 M	53 W	54 F	55 E
56 U	57 B	58 L	■	59 H	60 I	61 F	62 N	63 X	64 O	■	65 C	66 R	67 I	68 Q	69 B	70 L
71 Y	72 M	73 Z	■	74 I	75 J	76 W	77 Q	78 S	79 P	80 F	■	81 J	82 X	83 E	■	84 D
85 Y	■	86 C	87 W	88 R	89 F	90 M	91 L	92 P	■	93 B	94 N	95 S	■	96 Q	97 D	98 G
99 J	100 W	101 C	■	102 U	■	103 M	104 A	105 E	106 X	107 K	■	108 B	109 I	110 Z	111 F	112 G
■	113 U	114 L	■	115 V	116 A	■	117 N	118 P	119 W	■	120 J	121 U	122 F	■	123 Y	124 M
125 I	■	126 H	127 D	128 Z	129 G	130 B	131 K	132 Q	133 Z'	■	134 Z	135 V	136 O	137 M	138 I	139 A
140 X	141 N	142 R	143 Y	144 K	■	145 H	146 N	147 D	148 Z	■	149 Z'	150 L	151 I	152 A	153 B	154 Y
155 V	156 K	■	157 E	158 C	159 V	■	160 U	161 Q	162 Z'	163 F	164 Z'	165 X	■	166 K	167 Z	168 D
■	169 Y	170 M	171 L	172 N	173 E	174 O	■	175 F	176 I	177 Z	178 P	179 G	■	180 C	181 Q	182 R
■	183 K	184 F	185 G	186 A	187 Z'	■	188 Z'	189 P	190 M	191 R	192 A	193 Q	194 C	■	195 J	196 P
197 E	198 W	199 Z	200 T	■	201 C	202 F	203 W	■	204 K	205 V	206 N	■	207 G	208 H	209 A	210 Z'

C L U E S

A. Cut short
— 18 40 104 116 139 152 186 192 209

B. Characterized by intense agitation
— 57 69 93 108 130 153

C. Ad-lib (3 wds.)
— 158 180 194 201 86 101 4 30 65 17

D. Gave origin to; nurtured
— 27 45 38 84 97 127 147 168

E. Judgment of the Spanish Inquisition, followed by burning at the stake (comp.)
— 197 10 33 55 83 105 157 173

F. Locations for show windows
— 175 54 61 111 122 163 184 202 7 80 89

G. Forebrain and midbrain
— 98 112 129 179 31 47 185 207

H. City in northwest Syria
— 208 23 51 59 126 145

I. Censures, blames
— 151 176 11 60 74 109 125 138 48 67

W O R D S

J. Yellow, plumlike fruit of a tree, *Eriobotrya japonica*

$\overline{75}$ $\overline{99}$ $\overline{195}$ $\overline{42}$ $\overline{81}$ $\overline{120}$

K. Chitter-chatter, blah-blah (comp.)

$\overline{144}$ $\overline{166}$ $\overline{36}$ $\overline{107}$ $\overline{131}$ $\overline{183}$ $\overline{44}$ $\overline{156}$ $\overline{204}$ $\overline{5}$

L. Measuringworms

$\overline{91}$ $\overline{150}$ $\overline{171}$ $\overline{50}$ $\overline{58}$ $\overline{70}$ $\overline{114}$

M. One of the seven hills of Rome

$\overline{190}$ $\overline{21}$ $\overline{103}$ $\overline{124}$ $\overline{137}$ $\overline{170}$ $\overline{52}$ $\overline{72}$ $\overline{90}$

N. Summarize, reword

$\overline{146}$ $\overline{3}$ $\overline{14}$ $\overline{26}$ $\overline{62}$ $\overline{117}$ $\overline{141}$ $\overline{94}$ $\overline{172}$ $\overline{206}$

O. American playwright (1888–1959; *Anne of the Thousand Days*)

$\overline{13}$ $\overline{35}$ $\overline{174}$ $\overline{20}$ $\overline{64}$ $\overline{136}$ $\overline{162}$ $\overline{41}$

P. First strike for many a youthful angler

$\overline{178}$ $\overline{196}$ $\overline{79}$ $\overline{92}$ $\overline{118}$ $\overline{25}$ $\overline{189}$

Q. Jack Teagarden's instrument

$\overline{68}$ $\overline{161}$ $\overline{181}$ $\overline{77}$ $\overline{96}$ $\overline{193}$ $\overline{132}$ $\overline{12}$

R. Large wardrobe

$\overline{34}$ $\overline{191}$ $\overline{88}$ $\overline{66}$ $\overline{142}$ $\overline{182}$ $\overline{28}$

S. Back of the neck

$\overline{95}$ $\overline{39}$ $\overline{1}$ $\overline{49}$ $\overline{78}$

T. "In what distant ___ or skies" (Blake, "The Tyger")

$\overline{9}$ $\overline{15}$ $\overline{22}$ $\overline{43}$ $\overline{200}$

U. Mother, by Apollo, of Dorus, Laoducus, and Polypoetes

$\overline{160}$ $\overline{19}$ $\overline{56}$ $\overline{121}$ $\overline{113}$ $\overline{102}$

V. Skedaddles, clears out, splits (3 wds.)

$\overline{159}$ $\overline{2}$ $\overline{135}$ $\overline{29}$ $\overline{24}$ $\overline{16}$ $\overline{205}$ $\overline{115}$ $\overline{155}$

W. Panegyric, laudation

$\overline{76}$ $\overline{53}$ $\overline{198}$ $\overline{203}$ $\overline{119}$ $\overline{87}$ $\overline{46}$ $\overline{100}$

X. Perfumed

$\overline{32}$ $\overline{106}$ $\overline{63}$ $\overline{82}$ $\overline{165}$ $\overline{140}$ $\overline{8}$

Y. Pertaining to visual imagery clearly retained in the memory

$\overline{37}$ $\overline{71}$ $\overline{123}$ $\overline{85}$ $\overline{143}$ $\overline{154}$ $\overline{169}$

Z. Former province in Manchuria, capital Tsitsihar

$\overline{148}$ $\overline{128}$ $\overline{177}$ $\overline{199}$ $\overline{134}$ $\overline{6}$ $\overline{167}$ $\overline{73}$

Z¹. " 'Tis distance lends enchantment to ___" (2 wds.; Campbell, "Pleasures of Hope")

$\overline{133}$ $\overline{187}$ $\overline{110}$ $\overline{149}$ $\overline{164}$ $\overline{210}$ $\overline{188}$

■ S I X ■

Offshoots

The Double-Crostic has proved to be one of the most popular and durable offshoots of the crossword puzzle, but there have been many others. Several short-lived games cropped up during the crossword's heyday, from the late 1920's through the 1930's. One of the more curious was "Crossword Golf," invented by John Rebar. This hybrid combined the element of eighteen "holes" (diagrams) with the challenge of filling in the grids. The combination did not appeal to the average solver, however, and the game disappeared within the year. The hardier hybrids resulted from lucky coincidence rather than deliberate planning. The diagramless is one such survivor.

The diagramless was the product of an accident. Margaret Farrar, Prosper Buranelli and F. Gregory Hartswick met over lunch at Moneta's Restaurant in the Bowery one day in 1925, at the height of the crossword craze. They had brought along a stack of puzzles to proofread and approve. As they leafed through the pages, it soon became that obvious to them that one of the corresponding diagrams had been left behind. Hartswick quickly sketched a grid on the back of the menu. Using the clues as a guide, he found that the pattern could be reproduced easily as long as he filled in the numbers of each entry and penciled in black squares as he went along. This not only enabled him to check the clues, but, he discovered, even provided some extra fun as he re-created the diagram bit by bit. The collaborators decided to exploit this discovery, which they appropriately named the "diagramless."

Since the mid-1940's *The New York Times* has included a diagramless one Sunday a month on the puzzle page. Many regular crossword fans have expressed interest in it but cannot seem to grasp the technique, although Mrs. Farrar wrote a concise and helpful explanation on its mechanics in

February 1947. The first step is to determine the indicated size of the puzzle so as to establish an outer limit. In an average 21 × 21 puzzle the number of entries Down and Across usually reaches 140. If a 21 × 21 diagramless contains only about 100 entries, this means that more than the usual number of black squares will emerge in a zigzag pattern. Since an odd-shaped diagram cannot be easily predicted, the solver must prepare for a puzzle that will not conform to the square shape, but may have words separated by large blocks of dark squares.

Unlike the crossword, which can be attacked from any angle, the diagramless must be approached systematically, starting at 1 Across. In order to deduce the number of letters in the first Across answer, the solver must refer to the next entry. If it is 8 Across, the first word will, of course, contain seven letters. Once this is established, the Down entries will help to create a block of answers and set the puzzle on its path. Numbers should always be recorded as the puzzle progresses. Since the number of letters in a word is never indicated, the only way to gauge the answer is by cross-checking with the Down entries.

If the number of the second entry Across is not included in the Down column, it should be placed directly beneath 1 Across. But if the figure appears in both directions, it may be recorded to the right of 1 Across; sometimes, when the constructor feels particularly mischievous, it may appear way to the left and below 1 Across. Since tricks of this sort cannot be anticipated, a second sheet of graph paper for experiments may be in order until a general pattern is established. Rule of thumb dictates that each numbered square that is keyed Across and Down should have a black square both to its left and above it. Entries that work only Across end with a black square, while the exclusively Down entries have a black square above them.

The foresighted solver notes his answers next to the clues and then scans the definitions before attempting to re-create the diagram. Sometimes islands of answers may be uncovered in this way and united later; it is often useful to work out different sections on separate sheets of paper. Only confirmed diagramless fanatics try to establish the pattern before working the clues. The real fun lies in coordinating the two elements. For the beginner, Mrs. Farrar suggested practicing with a regular crossword by folding over the diagram and approaching the puzzle as a diagramless.

Although diagramless puzzles appeared early in the Simon and Schuster series, the form has never captured the crossword-loving masses. Experts in the field agree that the paperwork the puzzle entails has limited its audience. Will Weng feels that it requires too much extra effort; the solver is working not only to uncover words but also to establish the underlying pattern. Juggling words and numbers can be frustrating until the solver masters the technique. As the comic Henry Morgan once observed, "Diagramless puzzles are for people who are unable to leave the house." Nevertheless, the diagramless has its supporters and is still with us (Figs. 45 and 46).

By all odds, the most successful crossword offshoot has been Scrabble®. In the early 1930's, Alfred Butts, a New York architect who found time heavy on his hands during the Depression, invented what he called Criss-Cross, a board game combining elements of the crossword and the anagram. After experimenting with different combinations, he came up with a satisfactory formula: two to four players would create grids resembling crossword puzzles. The playing board would consist of a 225-square grid with sixty specially marked squares signifying bonus scores, and each player would use lettered tiles marked with numerical values to form vertical and horizontal interlocking words. To tally the score, the values of the letters were combined with the corresponding board bonuses. The player with the largest number of points would win. Confident that the product would sell, Butts set out to present it to several New York toy manufacturers.

To his astonishment, not one company expressed interest. Perhaps the presentation misled the manufacturers; the cardboard tiles seemed shoddy to the professional eye. Perhaps it was because crosswords were no longer considered big time. For a while, Butts flirted with the idea of manufacturing the game himself, but as economic conditions improved and more building began, he returned to his profession. However, he and his wife and friends continued to play his game over the years; as its reputation spread, he made about five hundred sets for private customers.

The story of Scrabble® would have ended at this point had it not been for James Brunot, who for years had been playing Criss-Cross with the Buttses. In 1948, when Brunot decided to retire from his position as executive director of the President's War Relief Control Board, he wanted to move to the country where he and his wife could set up a small business. The nature of the business had never been clear to him, but now he had a sudden brainstorm: he would manufacture Criss-Cross. After all, there had always been some demand for sets among those who had played the game. He approached Butts, and Butts agreed to relinquish his rights for a small percentage. During this transaction, the name Scrabble® was suggested, and a trademark was taken out under that label.

After moving to Newtown, Conneticut (population 782), the Brunots set up their Scrabble® business. Different parts of the game were ordered from different manufacturers, and the sets were assembled in their living room. Promotion was limited to small ads in such publications as *The Saturday Review* and *The Smith College Alumnae Quarterly*; in addition, each set included postcards for owners who wished to pass the word on to their friends. During 1949, their first year in business, the Brunots sold 2,251 games at a loss of $450. They lost money every subsequent year until 1952 when sales leaped from the January figure of 18 sets a day to 411, apparently as a result of word of mouth.

The summer of 1952 proved to be crucial for Scrabble®. Scores of players brought their sets along on vacation, and Scrabble® after dinner became as popular as dessert. Among those introduced to the game in this way was Jack Straus, owner of Macy's. He enjoyed the game so much that when he returned to the city he ordered a set from Macy's toy department. Upon being told that they had none, he demanded that they stock up at once. Before long, Macy's was in the vanguard of Scrabble® outlets in New York City. Other summer players put their names on waiting lists at their local toy stores. Although New York City and the North Side of Chicago were the first to fall in line, demand began to sweep other parts of the country.

The Brunots returned from a week's vacation to discover 2,500 orders instead of the expected 250. Friends were recruited to help out; the living room was overrun with scattered parts and people. Soon the Brunot company had to move to a converted schoolhouse down the road. At the new location thirty-five employees working in two shifts endeavored to produce 6,000 sets a week. As the demand continued to increase, Brunot decided it was time to go to a large manufacturer. Just as he came to this conclusion, Selchow & Righter, the makers of Parcheesi, as well as the suppliers of the Scrabble® boards over the years, approached him. A deal was signed in February 1953, with Brunot receiving five percent of the wholesale price.

The Selchow & Righter takeover coincided with the March 1953 Toy Fair held in New York City. Orders poured in at such a rate that they were unable to keep up with the enormous demand. Sets were distributed in monthly installments to the various stores. By October, the year's supplies were depleted. The Macy's buyer asked that the exact delivery date of the next supply be reported early enough to arrange for a full-page ad in *The*

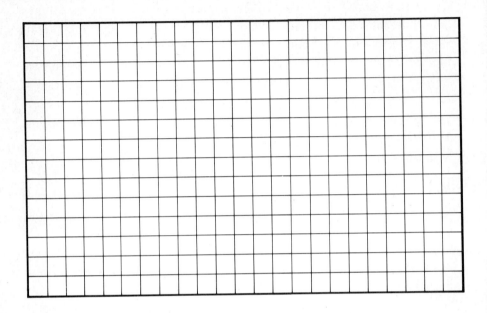

1 Social harmony
7 State over the border
11 Freight car monogram
14 —— Felix
15 Antique shop item
16 Ruff
17 —— *of the North* (movie)
18 Caesar and tossed
20 College at Storrs
22 Busy one
23 Bowler at times
25 Chinese gift
26 Writer James and family
29 Agreed
32 Change
33 Where's the —— telephone?
35 City on the Connecticut
37 Kind of increment
41 Hindu title of respect
42 Snow in the Pyrenees
43 Vigor's companion
46 Gypsy
49 Packers
51 —— majesté
52 Suffix with station
53 Into the —— of the gale
54 Dressed
56 —— de deux
57 Impervious
60 —— event or report
62 Kind of card, for short
64 Heard at the Capitol
67 Caprice
68 Boccaccio's tales
69 Not "it"
70 Chris
71 Montezuma, e.g.
72 City on the Sound
73 Gull and osprey ——
74 More or ——

D O W N

1 Famous trial locale
2 Anita's favorite color
3 French cape
4 Kwa language
5 Spanish uncle
6 Butter producers
7 Riot
8 Prize
9 But, to Cicero
10 Old folks: Abbr.
11 Quick!
12 "——— unto Caesar"
13 Jacques's fox
18 Amerind
19 Light
20 ——— the crack of dawn
21 The Baalites' golden ———
24 Israel Putnam, e.g.
27 Sea denizen
28 Holy ———
30 Syllables of hesitation
31 Women's organization

34 South Carolina river
36 Connecticut ———
38 Yale's city
39 Night before
40 Maddens
44 Verb suffix
45 Kind of practice
46 Is sorry
47 Spanish tennis player
48 Whalers' port
49 Felt
50 Royal family
51 Tomlin
53 Piano man
55 Knave of Hearts theft
57 Paragraph
58 Upset
59 S.E. Asian
61 Church part
63 Nap
64 ——— and ahs
65 Decay
66 Wine vessel

F I G U R E 46 ▪ *Diagramless 17 × 15 by Norton Rhoades. Printed by kind permission of the author.*

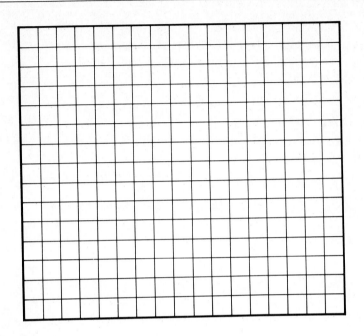

8 Certain corner
9 Pleasant edge
10 Before
12 One of the Gershwins
13 One living with another
15 Turkish or Irani tribesman
16 Thought: Prefix
17 Where Sappho wrote
19 Entertainment complex
22 Sold
24 Cutting ties
27 Getting along in years
28 Hair or lip features
29 Inter ———
30 Deck feature
32 Cheats

33 Rake
35 Ancient literary language
37 Mix
39 Sometimes a rooster
40 Purposes
41 Utter
44 Frog comment
45 Hercules' captive
46 Old-time auto
47 Better than none
48 ——— bene
49 Amor
50 To ——— (exact): Var.
52 Baden-Baden
54 46D, e.g.
55 Begin's land: Abbr.

New York Times. This event occurred just in time for the Memorial Day weekend, causing a sensation in the metropolitan area.

Nineteen fifty-four was a record year, with 1955 a close second. Day and night shifts at Selchow & Righter's Brooklyn factory churned out sets. In two years Scrabble® managed to join Parcheesi as one of the all-time best-selling games. Meanwhile, in Newtown, Brunot was making handsome deluxe leather-encased sets; even these, priced at ten dollars each, were selling like hot cakes. Brunot also continued to receive stacks of letters, many of them requests for new tiles to replace those that had been swallowed by pet dogs. Apparently the chemical on the tiles provided a delectable treat to many discerning canine palates. Other tiles were lost at the beach. "Jones Beach must be paved with them," Brunot mused at one point.

By 1957, Travel Scrabble® and Revolving Scrabble® were added to the line. Scrabble® for Juniors appeared in 1958. This spin-off was the result of a meeting in which a buyer remarked that his little girl was anxious to grow up in order to be able to play Scrabble®. Brunot was consulted, and requested only that the juvenile version adhere to the original standards of the game. For children, the board was altered, and words were actually spelled out on the grid as a spelling aid. Each player simply matched a tile with a letter on the board. For older players, there was a blank side on the reverse of the board so that they could play a version closer to the adult game. Eventually twenty-two versions of the game appeared in six languages and the whole world became involved in the Scrabble® epidemic.

Inevitably, Scrabble® tournaments were organized. In 1973 they were officially united under the aegis of Scrabble® Word Games, Inc., whose president and executive director, James Houle (a chemical engineer by trade), oversees the various competitions and arbitrates long-distance controversies. There are more than one hundred clubs in the United States and Canada, with some 10,000 members. A bimonthly newsletter keeps the players up-to-date on tips and helpful facts and provides notes on useful words.

To make the most of any Scrabble® hand, experts recommend the following: (1) balance your tiles by building a good mix of vowels and consonants and avoiding double consonants; (2) save potential suffixes and prefixes such as -ing, -tion, -est; (3) try to make "hook words," which can be retooled later, such as the addition of "e" to "gam" in order to form "game"; (4) go for bonus boxes at all costs; (5) expand your vocabulary by memorizing useful short words. To open the game, the best strategic move is to use the largest possible number of tiles; single-letter plays are considered beginner tactics.

Two Chicago Scrabble® sharks, Nick Ballard and Joseph Cortese, have collaborated on various lists of bingo words, compiling fragments of six letters that combine successfully with a seventh letter. One valuable sequence of letters is contained in the word "satire," whose letters can join with at least seventeen other letters to create a word. For example, with the letter "l" satire can become an anagram for "retails," with "b" "baiters," and so on. Three words with colossal bingo potential if the letters are placed in strategic positions are "bezique," "mezquite," and "quetzals." An expert player will try for a bingo within the first four moves and then again in the last four out of a game of about fifteen plays. Use of the term "bingo" has been open to debate, since it seems to imply a gamble rather than skill. Fans have suggested the term "scrabble" instead, or even "slam."

When preparing for tournaments, some sharks like to hone their talents by working crossword puzzles. Carl Dalke, an Illinois champion, feels that this may be a mixed blessing since crosswords contain too many proper names and words that are illegal in Scrabble®. However, other experts feel that crosswords offer an opportunity to build greater word expertise, especially in words of seven letters. Both pastimes feed the same desire to play with language by fitting words into geometric frames. Elliot Avedon, curator of the only known Museum and Archive of Games, which is located at the University of Waterloo in Ontario where he is also a professor of recreation, views the situation in this way: "Scrabble® and crosswords are modern games because they reflect a love of language instead of symbols."

The electronic Scrabble-type game Sensor added a new dimension to word games in 1979. The old-fashioned board game was preempted by a sleek battery-operated computer that features a twenty-six-button alphabet keyboard. By programming a secret word into its memory bank, one player can engage another in a deductive search; the answer may contain from two to seven letters. The seeker then punches guesses into the keyboard and watches for results on a display panel. Twelve tries is the maximum, after which the score is tallied and positions switched. For truly avid Sensor players, a game of solitaire can be arranged by directing the computer to program its own hidden word.

Another addictive game for the word-game fan is Boggle, a Parker Brothers Hidden Word Game. Sixteen lettered cubes are jumbled and then arranged into fitted squares. A timer allows players three minutes to list

A C R O S S

1 One of the 3 bears
5 Steeds
10 Tundra homes: var.
15 Idaho farmer's output
19 Vaccine or history
20 Star in "The 39 Steps"
21 Western prop
22 Folk dance in Haifa
23 Ninotchka's distant relation?
25 Gingerbread man's parent?
27 Appliances
28 Bea Arthur role
30 Canto; division
31 French zoo attraction
32 Trump card in some games
33 Fast season
34 Discharge
37 Actor-director Tom
38 Brown's headquarters
42 St. ——— Cathedral, London
43 Davis to Balzac, in English though
45 Morgue, for one
46 Poker player's delight
47 Hot or big
48 Deli sign
49 Centerpiece, often
50 66, for example
51 Brady Bunch siblings?
55 Leonine
56 Least resonant
58 April days, generally
59 With an imperious air
60 South American tea leaves
61 Dieter's undoing
62 Tragedian's theme
63 Garden tool
65 Urgency
66 Lawn
69 Particles

70 Ugly Duckling's parent?
72 Methylbenzene: comb. form
73 Where the Eder flows
74 Pome fruit variety
75 Tubers
76 Indian title
77 Deplete, with up
78 Teddy's sibling?
82 Gams
83 Long hairs
85 Society members
86 Yes or no follow-up
87 Basics
88 Ford to family
89 Got it ———
90 Sibyl
93 Emulated Marceau
94 Taboo
98 Referee's parent?
100 Mrs. Eisenhower to some?
102 Manicurist's tool
103 Like some furniture
104 Latter-day crusader
105 Iroquois tribe
106 Skirt feature
107 Refine
108 Jennie Lind was one
109 Glean

D O W N

1 Bratty expression
2 Tuscan river
3 Inca's transport
4 Certain Day
5 Consider; heed
6 Thunders
7 Raggedy and Cape
8 Window style
9 Flower parts
10 Metabolic regulator
11 Cheese tray item
12 Peanut gallery
13 Sweatshirt emblem for Heiden
14 Garden dwellers
15 California volcano
16 Where peas are found
17 Pakistani tongue
18 "Happy ———"
24 Sewing kits
26 Beatrice's admirer
29 Prefix for meter
32 Seizures
33 Lithuanian cousins
34 In different worlds
35 Peyote sources
36 Hive leader to swarm?
37 Appoint
38 Arctic pioneer
39 Alarm clock's ancestor?
40 European blackbird: var.
41 Like a ragamuffin
43 Fischer's forte
44 Designer Geoffrey
47 Type of band or blue
49 Jeeves, to some
51 Builder's considerations
52 Eyes of song
53 À votre ——— !
54 Blake's metaphor
55 Monk, in Lyons
57 Pilot's aid
59 Vexed
61 Cookie unit
62 Imitate a laden table
63 Pancake enhancer: var.
64 Seven Gables is one
65 Armies
66 Actress Nina and French general
67 Crooner Eydie
68 Beethoven wrote for her
70 Satellites
71 Awkward
74 Mexican laborers
76 Crepe paper creation
78 Old or New Testament
79 Sodium
80 Bergsonian term
81 Hamilton and Barbara
82 Advance furtively
84 Fragrance
86 Horatian output
88 Hebrew letter
89 Pastel-like
90 Rubs out
91 Measure of thinness
92 Gudrun's husband
93 Television personality Douglas
94 Riviera wave
95 Goods
96 Having blood: comb. form
97 Like still waters
99 Headwear in the Highlands
101 Detroit org.

words of three or more letters. After some practice the player's eye begins to weave words together, skillfully connecting diagonal letters to create seven- or even eight-letter words.

With all these advances in the world of word games, it is no wonder the crossword puzzle has become a permanent fixture in modern culture. Since it regained popularity during World War II, its survival has never been in doubt. Moving ever farther away from its early days as a dictionary exercise, the crossword has come to stand for an obsessive quest. As clues have grown more clever and deceptive, a sort of code has evolved that requires practice and a certain turn of mind. Without this inside information, the crossword puzzle often appears enigmatic and inscrutable. Archaeologist Iris Love, recognizing this deductive process, has compared her own work to solving a crossword puzzle. And in discussing the intricate plots of Dorothy Sayers's novels, author Simon Brett remarked, "I thought those books needed a crossword-puzzle type of mind."

The 1913 American newspaper filler that eleven years later helped to launch the publishing house of Simon and Schuster has become an international password, from the French *Mots Croisés* to the Spanish *Crucigramas* to the German *Kreuzworträtsel* to the Soviet *Krestoslovitsa*. Generations of solvers in all nations who have mastered the 15 × 15 dailies have gone on to explore the 21 × 21 and 23 × 23 Sunday puzzles. Crossword-solving has even been sanctioned by educators, who view it as a tool in vocabulary building, thus ensuring a place for the puzzles in most grammar-school publications. And yet, the true value of the crossword remains the complete distraction it offers from the anxieties of daily life. By presenting a solvable problem, the puzzle offers comfort to a chaotic world. Over the years Margaret Farrar has observed that crossword-puzzle books tend to sell better during times of economic crisis. She believes that this is because when money is scarce, the crossword represents a hurdle that can be conquered. Besides, she adds, "Who can worry about the rent when you're trying to solve 25 Down?" (Fig. 47).

P U Z Z L E
S O L U T I O N S

Note: There are no solutions to Figs. 3, 7, 8

F I G U R E 1

KISS

F I G U R E 2

Answer to rebus:

The Enigma is of such ancient and remarkable origin, that I shall ask no one to excuse me for offering this book to the public. Enigmatical questions are frequent in the Scriptures, and in olden times often contained a great deal of valuable information.

I intend, my dear young friends, to combine instruction with amusement; and do not fear but what my expectations will be sufficiently realized.

Right well, I know, little lads and lasses, you cannot fail to be delighted when I am making such efforts in your behalf; so, heartily shaking you all by the band, I remain—

Yours truly,

AUNT SUE

F I G U R E 4

TABLECLOTH

T	uni	C
A	nge	L
B	at	O
L	ocus	T
E	lija	H

F I G U R E 5

EARNESTLY

FIGURE 6

PROVERB REBUS. An empty bag cannot stand upright.

CONCEALED BIRDS. 1. Eagle. 2. Nightingale. 3. Heron. 4. Swan. 5. Hawk. 6. Hen.
7. Lark 8. Flamingo. 9. Ostrich. 10. Dodo. 11. Dove. 12. Pewit. 13. Owl. 14. Emu.

CROSS-WORD ENIGMA. Cowper.

DICKENS DOUBLE ACROSTIC. Primals: Bagstock (Dombey and Son). Finals: Traddles
(David Copperfield). Cross-words: 1. BagneT (Bleak House). 2. AggerawayteR (Tale of
Two Cities). 3. GeorgianA (Mutual Friend). 4. Small-weeD (Bleak House). 5. TrotwooD
(David Copperfield). 6. Old BilL (Great Expectations). 7. CuttlE (Dombey and Son).
8. KenwigS (Nicholas Nickleby).

NUMERICAL OMISSIONS. Pepper-grass.

THREE EASY DIAMONDS. I. 1. T. 2. HUb. 3. TuRin. 4. BIg. 5. N. II. 1. H. 2. DOg.
3. HoUnd. 4. GNu. 5. D. III. 1. L. 2. COw. 3. LoUis. 4.WIt. 5. S.

PICTORIAL NUMERICAL ENIGMA. A Merry Christmas and a Happy New Year.

CONNECTED DIAMONDS. Centrals across: Break-water. Left-hand Diamond: 1. B. 2. ORe.
3. BrEak. 4. EAt. 5. K. Right-hand Diamond: 1. W. 2. LAw. 3. WaTer. 4. WEt. 5. R.

THREE NUMERICAL ENIGMAS. I. Tarpaulin. II. Lady Jane Grey. III. Combatable.

EASY DOUBLE ACROSTIC. Primals: Santa. Finals: Claus. Cross-words: 1. ScholastiC.
2. AccidentaL. 3. NebraskA. 4. TableaU. 5. AnonymouS.

FIGURE 9

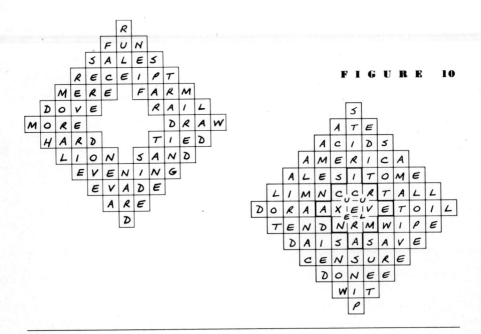

FIGURE 10

FIGURE 11

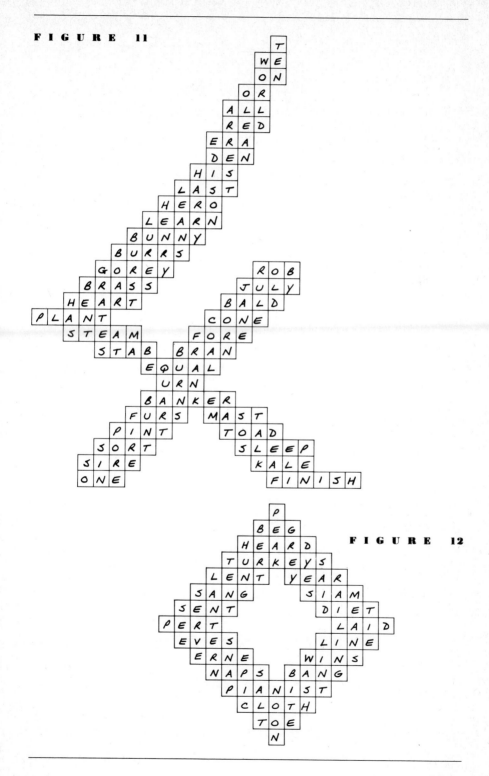

FIGURE 13

FIGURE 14

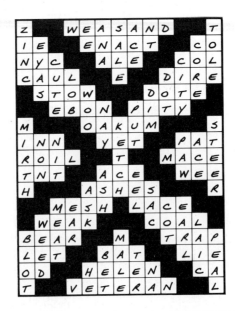

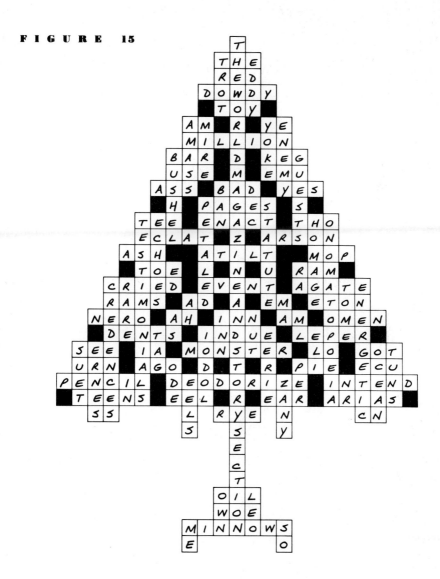

FIGURE 16

```
    O S S I A   C R U D E
  A L M O N D   A U R E R S
G L E E   S M A R T   N O O N
A D O L F   I D A   A I S L E
N O   T A U R I F O R M   D E
A S E   C R A T E R S   P E D
M E N S U A L   S C E N E R Y
  D O L L       A N I L
A M E N T I A   S N I P E R S
M O D   A T T U N E D   E A T
O Z   S T E A R A T E S   T O
R A K E E   V A G   S E R I R
T R O T   B I L G E   P I N E
  T I T H E S   E R R I N G
  R O A S T   D R E A D
```

FIGURE 19

```
S W I T H E R G E A C H
P A J O C K O I L P I E
O L O B I O S P O U N D
S T U A R T E S R O C S
H E N C O S T Y A C H T
A R C C I S T S P A D E
S H E O L A A E R I N E
P A S S D N E P I L I V
I M P E N D N S N O S E
```

FIGURE 20

```
S M E A R   P E N S E R O S O
  A   B   M A Y O   V   S   D
N O M A D   R E S P E C T E D
  R   S E W   D E A N   L   I
D I E H A R D   S U S P E C T
E   R E L I E F   S O A R   Y
S K I D   T U R E E N S
K   N   A   C O N   G   S   D
    I M M E N S E   A L T O
B   U M B O   T U R T L E   O
R A S P I N G   E A R L D O M
I   E   T A R A   S E E   P
D I F F I D E N T   E G R E T
E   U   O   E N I D   R   R
S E L E N I T E S   T O T A L
```

FIGURE   21

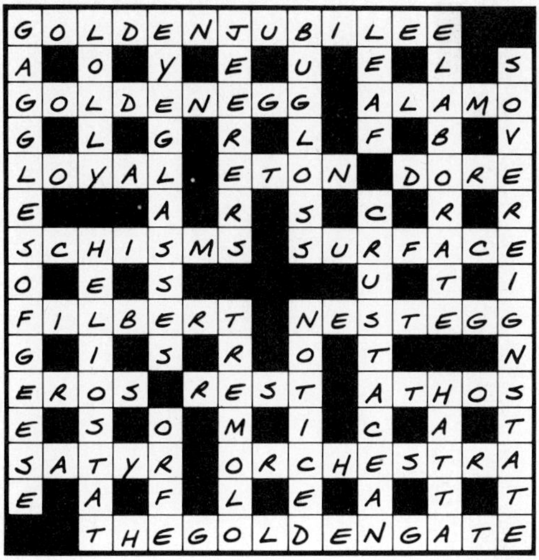

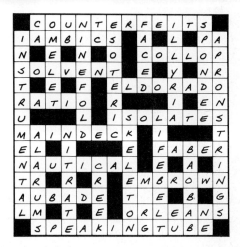

FIGURE   22

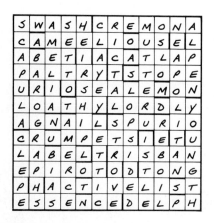

FIGURE   23

FIGURE 24

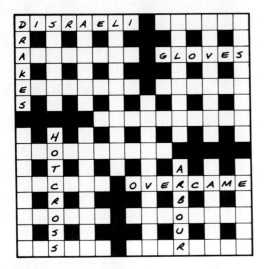

To better camouflage his bogus crossword, Beerbohm included six "genuine" clues:
1 *Across*, Disraeli (anagram); 1 *Down*, which refers to Newbolt's poem "Drake's Drum";
10 *Across*, gloves; 16 *Down*, hot cross; 23 *Across*, from Antony's funeral speech in *Julius Caesar*, overcame; 19 *Down*, harbour with the top cut off yields arbour. London *Times* crossword editor Edmund Akenhead suggests that there is yet a seventh answerable clue: 27 *Across*, praiseth (anagram). However, he points out, both 19 *Down* and 27 *Across* cannot both be right as they do not fit in with each other. But perhaps this was simply this constructor's way of further frustrating the solver.

FIGURE 25

T	A	L	B	A	T	S
H	T	E	E	T	W	A
E	I	T	A	H	A	P
R	B	O	T	C	P	B
E	A	O	R	T	I	A
M	H	C	I	I	T	S
A	D	E	N	G	O	T

FIGURE 26

The order of the letters within each diagram square is arbitrary.

BS	D/BE	R/T	A/G	N/RA	E/Y	T/S	
R/O	I/R	D/I	DL/F	L/I	ED/C	DE	EO
A/C	L/O	S	TU/E	M/N	ER/A	T/E	R
NR	GL	TK	SL	TS/E	EP	T/A	NE
D/A	E/LT	SK/O		SE	FL	OS	AH
I/TN	O/A	D/CU	Y/BA	I/N	A/T		G/E
SI	S/LU	AN/G	GR/GA	AG/I	E		A
H/C	O/A	NK/T	E/ER	RS/E	R		RD

Across. 2a. BET(RAY)S 2b. DRAGNET (anag.) 7a. RIDDLED (double def.) 7b. OR-IF-ICE 8a. COSTUMER (anag.) 8b. ALI-ENATE (*a teen* anag.) 10a. T(h)E-T(h)E 10b. SPAN (double def.) 12a. ALT-O ([*f*]*lat* anag.) 12b. DESK (hidden) 15a. IN-CUB(AT)E 15b. TO-A-DYING 16a. SANG-RIA (*air* rev.) 16b. LUG-GAG-E 17a. HON(K)ERS (anag. + *k*) 17b. CATERER (anag.) *Down.* 1a. SOCRATIC (anag.) 1b. BRAN-DISH 2a. DROL-L (*lord* rev.) 2b. BIL(G)E 3a. R-(IS)-K 3b. EDIT (rev.) 4a. G(L)UTS 4b. RINSE (anag.) 5a. AC(M)E 5b. NE(A)P (*pen* rev.; pun) 6a. TEENAGER (anag.) 6b. SOREHEAD (anag.) 9a. LODGE (double def.) 9b. SKUNK (double def.) 11a. TO(N)GS 11b. A-STIR 13a. SCAN(t) 13b. TAUT (homophone) 14a. FARE (double def.) 14b. LIAR (rev.)

FIGURE 27

D	A	N	G	E	R	G	M	R	I	F	F
I	N	E	R	T	D	I	U	R	N	A	L
R	O	A	N	U	I	N	S	E	C	T	A
T	I	T	L	I	N	G	T	C	L	S	N
Y	N	F	A	S	T	E	A	L	I	N	G
S	T	U	T	T	E	R	R	A	N	G	E
E	A	R	T	H	R	E	D	R	E	S	S
T	O	L	E	R	A	N	T	E	D	E	S
T	F	O	R	O	S	T	A	T	U	R	E
L	I	N	E	U	P	S	N	D	R	A	W
E	N	G	A	G	E	D	G	R	A	P	E
R	E	S	T	H	D	B	O	I	L	E	D

The fourteen asterisked clues led to answers that directed solvers to perform an additional operation: anagramming. For example, Shakespeare *directed solvers to anagram* speare *for the final answer,* serape.

Across. *1. ROCK GARDEN (anag.) 7. RIFF (double def.) *11. INTERCHANGED (anag.) 12. DI(URN)AL 13. R(O)AN 14. IN-SECT-A 15. TIT-LING *19. MARTIN-GALES (hidden) 20. ST(art)-UTTER 22. RANGE (double def.) *23. HEARTBROKEN (anag.) 24. REDRESS (double def.) 26. TOLERANT (anag.) *30. ILLUSTRATE (anag.) 32. LINE-UPS 33. DRAW (double def.) 34. ENG(lish)-AGED 35. GR-APE *36. SPINST(E)R (anag. + *e*) 37. B(OIL)ED *Down.* 1. DIRTY (anag.) *2. ALTERNATION (anag.) *3. CAST-A-NET 4. ETUIS (anag.) *5. BADGE-RING 6. M(US-TAR)D 8. IN(CLI)N-ED *9. BREAK-FAST 10. F-LANGES (anag. + *f*) *16. RATTLESNAKES (anag.) 17. C-LARET (anag. + *c*) 18. FUR(LONG)S *20. NEWSLETTER (anag.) 21. TH(e)-ROUGH 24. RASPED (anag.) *25. SHAKESPEARE (anag.) 27. TAN-GO *28. TUMBLEWEEDS (anag.) 29. FINE (double def.) 31. URAL (hidden)

FIGURE 28

```
 S A M E     O P A L
 T A M E R   N A S A L
 H E M ■ W A G E R ■ M A T
 O P U S         S I T E
 P E E L         K N E E
   E L I         E A R
       P         W
   M A P         E R G
 T O L E         R E L Y
 H O L D         S T O A
 E R E ■ A D A M S ■ O A K
   S Y R I A   A P O R T
   S P R Y     R A F T
```

FIGURE 29

```
   S T E A L S ■ E M
   W I L S O N ■ L A
   E N S ■ N A M E S
   A T E ■ E P I C S
 B E T S         T I D E
 R E ■           O V E R
 A R C H         R E N O
 T I R O       ■ I S
 S E E S         T A M E
   A T O N E ■ E R R
   T I B E R ■ R U E
   E L ■ S I L I C A
   D E ■ T E A S E S
```

F I G U R E 30

```
O P P           I R E
A R A B     P U S     S C A R
T O R I C   D A R T S   S T O N E
  D E P O S E R ■ O P U L E N T
    D O R I C S   R A Z O R S
    L A ■ K O R A N ■ G I
  S A L T ■ N A G ■ W A L I
P E R S O N S   E M I N E N T
A L ■   N I ■   O S ■   A U
C A R T E L S   N A P P I N G
  H E R S ■ C O O ■ S I N E
    C A ■ C A R V E ■ A T
    P I S T O L ■ I R O N E D
  C A T H O D E   C O R O N A S
H O N E Y   A N D E S   S T I L E
I C E S     E O S     S L O T
M A D             Y E A
```

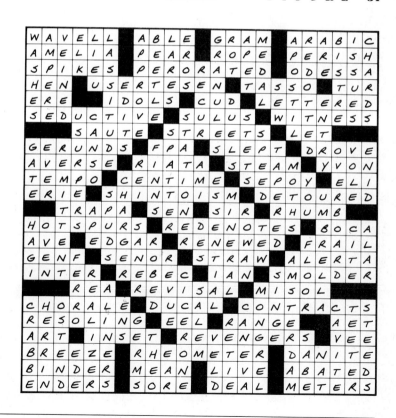

FIGURE   34

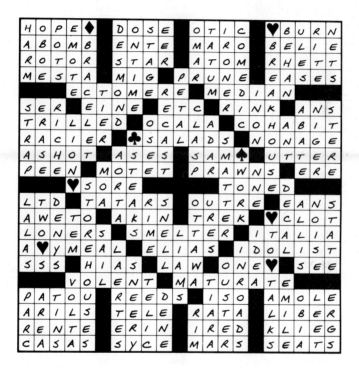

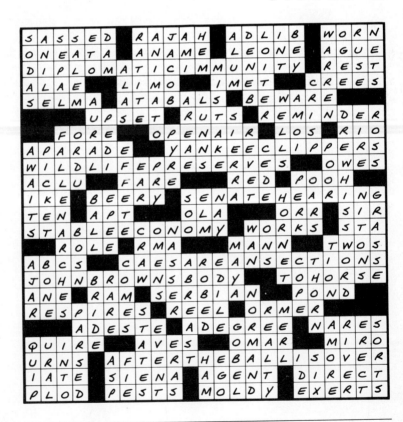

```
M A D A M I S O G A M Y
A R A G O N I T E K Y R
R A T A N A M I S E R E
K L U M A C R O L E I N
H E R I O T C S S P O T
O V A D P I L E W O R T
R I G A D O O N E B A R
N A M E R N S A L A M I
A T O M I S E R C L A S
T H R I V E T I H A D E
E A R S E L E N I T I C
S N A R L E D D E A L T
```

Across:
1 mad *plus* ami
2 misogamy
10 *anag* ie tango *in* ark
11 ratan; *see* rattan (1)
12 er *in* a mise, & *lit*
14 lei *in* macron
15 riot *in* hec(k)
17 ss *plus* pot
18 trowel *plus* I *plus* pd *rev*
20 rig *plus* a *plus* do *plus* one
23 namer
24 *anag*
25 miser *in* atoc
28 th(e) rivet
29 had *in* ie
30 *comp anag*
31 sn *plus* a *plus* L *in* redd
32 deal *in* DT

Down:
1 mark *plus* horn
2 a *plus* tu(g) *in* drag
3 a *plus* dim *plus* a *in* a *plus* gem
4 a *in* mono
5 *anag*
6 (u)se *in* (m)otion
7 a *plus* keep
8 o *plus* ram *in* myriad
9 yr *in* ent(t)
13 a *plus* tha(r) *in* alevin
16 clos(e) *in* deter *rev*
17 h *plus* clews *rev, in* lie
19 tri ('try') *plus* sec *in* TT
21 pd *plus* rive *plus* £
22 ob. *plus* alat(e) *plus* a: bullet-head
23 *anag. & lit*
26 morra: *see* mora (2)
27 N(itrogen) *in* arid

Across:

1 SCRUB. *Anagram* clue. The word
CURBS anagrammed ("messy") makes
SCRUB ("to clean").

4 MINOR. *Reversal* clue. MINOR ("not yet
twenty-one") is RON I'M spelled
backwards. The reversal is indicated
by "Come back."

5 AMEND. *Container* clue. AMEND
("change") consists of MEN ("the
males") inside AD ("commercial").

Down:

1 SAMOA. *Concealed word* clue. SAMOA
("an island") is concealed in "there'S
A MOAt."

2 RANGE. *Second definition* clue. RANGE
is both a stove and an extent.

3 BORED. *Homonym* clue. BORED
("tired") sounds the same as BOARD
("inn's meals"). The homonym is
indicated by the words "we hear."

C R O S S W O R D   À   L ' A N G L A I S E

Across:

1 Antelope (ante + lope)
5 Airman (marina)
9 Twice-Told (twice-tolled)
11 Droll (D + roll)
12 Cute (cut + e)
13 Injunction (in junction)
15 Appears (AP + pears)
17 Litter
19 Gemini (e.g. + mini)
20 Drowsed (sword + Ed)
22 Chef's salad (calf dashes)
23 Okra (o.k. + ra)
26 Revue (rue + Ev)
27 Existence (e + x + is + ten +Ce)
28 Easily (Yale is)
29 Ignorant (ranting + O)

Down:

1 Autocrat (auto + car + T)
2 Taint ('taint!)
3 Leer (reel)
4 Prognosticate (operating cost)
6 Indication (vindication − v)
7 Moodiness (moos + dines)
8 Nylons (viNYL ON shower)
10 Double-dealing
14 Magic spell (is leg-clamp)
16 Preserves
18 Adjacent (a d.j. + a cent)
21 Accrue (a crew)
24 Kenya (stricKEN YAnkee)
25 Otto (to + to)

FIGURE 39

```
P A T S   B A C H       C L A M       T M A N
E R I C   L I R E   H A I T I   T H E N Y
A L T O   O R E M   O R L O N   R E S T E
S O O T C A S E S   G R I M E B O S S E S
    T O T   D I R G E     D E L T A S
U N F I R E D   N E A R S   S L A M
C A L E N D E R   F R A U G H T   T E L
L S U     L I B     N R A   X E R E S
A T E N O C L O C K S Q U A L O R   I T I
    E R L   B E A T U P   F L A C C I D
S O M E B O D Y   R I O   F A S T L A N E
E R U D I T E   M O N T R E   E E E
R O C   T H E F I L T H A M E N D M E N T
A N K A S   R U N     G U Y     R E A
  O Y L   S E L K I R K   R E M E D I A L
  M A S T   S N E E S   D U R A N T E
  B A S H E D   S C A L E   L A W
R A N K A N D V I L E   O B J E T D I R T
A S T A R   A R E A S   P O E T   L E A R
M I L N E   Y A R N S   P L E A   E R I E
S E E S     S I E G   Y I P S   D I D Y
```

FIGURE 40

Alfred Lord Tennyson: "*Ulysses*"
And tho
We are not now that strength which in old days
Moved earth and heaven, that which we are, we are.
One equal temper of heroic hearts,
Made weak by time and fate, but strong in will
To strive, to seek, to find and not to yield.

FIGURE 41

Chesterton: *A Defense of Slang*
The Americans have an expression "swelled head" as a description of self-approval. An American said that after the Chinese War the Japanese wanted "to put on their hats with a shoehorn." This is a monument of the true nature of slang.

Inez H. Irwin: *The Californiacs*
He grows restive the instant you get off the subject of California. On the other hand, that frenzied patriotism has its wonderful and beautiful side. . . California is quite as beautiful as her poets insist and her painters prove.

Hemingway: *The Old Man and The Sea*
He is a great fish and I must convince him, he thought. I must never let him learn his strength nor what he could do if he made his run. . . But, thank God, they are not as intelligent as we who kill them; although they are more noble and able.

Thomas Carlyle: *Past and Present*
Quack and Dupe . . . are. . . of the self-same substance; . . . turn up your dupe into the proper fostering element, and he himself can become a quack; there is in him the due prurient insincerity, open voracity for profit, and closed sense for truth, whereof quacks, too. . . are made.

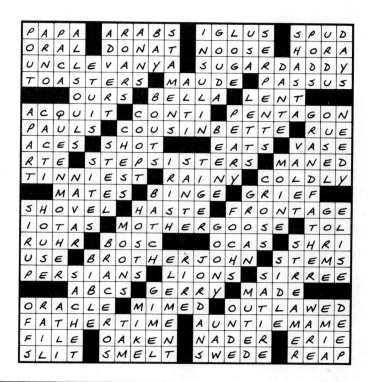

▪ BIBLIOGRAPHY ▪

BOOKS

Bellamy, William. *Broken Words*. Boston: Houghton Mifflin Co., 1911.

Bombaugh, C. *Gleanings for the Curious*. Chicago: A.D. Worthington & Co., 1875.

Buranelli, Prosper, et al. *The Celebrity Cross Word Puzzle Book*. New York: Simon and Schuster, 1925.

Disraeli, Isaac. *Curiosities of Literature*. New York: Sheldon & Co., 1862.

Eastern Puzzlers' League. *Key to Puzzledom*. New York: W. Delaney, 1906.

Encyclopaedia Britannica. "Crossword Puzzle," volume 6, page 816, 1972.

Farrar, Margaret, ed. *Simon and Schuster Crossword Puzzle Book Series 100*. New York: Simon and Schuster, 1974.

Hill, Norman. *How to Solve Crossword Puzzles*. New York: Funk & Wagnall's, 1974.

Hovanec, Helene. *The Puzzler's Paradise*. New York: Paddington Press, 1978.

Macnutt, D. S. *Ximenes on the Art of the Crossword Puzzle*. London: Methuen, 1966.

Millington, Roger. *Crossword Puzzles: Their History and Cult*. New York: Nelson, 1974.

The Modern Sphinx. London: Griffith & Farran, 1873.

National Puzzlers' League. *Real Puzzles*. New York: W. Delaney, 1925.

————, *New Primer of Puzzledom*. New York: W. Delaney, 1958.

Pearson, A. Cyril. *Pictured Puzzles and Word Play*. New York: Routledge, 1908.

Penguin Book of Sunday Times Crosswords. New York: Penguin Books, 1978.

Penguin Book of The Times 50th Anniversary Crosswords. New York: Penguin Books, 1980.

Rebar, J. N., et al. *Cross-Word Golf*. New York: Dutton, 1933.

ARTICLES

Ackerman, John. "He's Never at a Loss for Words: Eugene Maleska." *Sunday Standard-Times* (Wareham, Mass.), 27 July 1976.

American Heritage. "Crosswords in History." October 1976, 27:100.

Baker, Russell. "Crashing Into Crossword Land." *The New York Times*, 19 January 1975.

Bell, Robert. "The End of the Crossword?" *Fortnightly*, April 1937, 147:476–80.

Buranelli, Prosper, et al. "How the Crossword Craze Started, by the Starters." *Colliers*, 31 January 1925, 75:12.

Clark, Mary E. "Editorial Forum: Crossword Puzzle Contests vs. The Public Library." *Library JournalM*, 15 February 1935, 60:152.

Cort, David. "The Crossword Addict." *The Nation*, 29 July 1961, 193:54–7.

Current Literature. "The Puzzle Habit." July 1901, 31:73.

Dudar, Helen. "Margaret Farrar." Original manuscript, Writer's Bloc, 1978.

Dunn, Dooley. "Get it? Ha, ha!" *The New York Times*, 21 March 1943, p. 59.

Ephron, Nora. "Working the Double-Crostic." *Esquire*, May 1977, 87:10.

Farrar, Margaret. "Move As If Driven." *The New York Times*, 2 February 1947.

———, "Guest Word: A Puzzlement." *The New York Times*, 7 April 1974.

Fried, Eunice. "Getting Down and Across." *American Way*, February 1979, pp. 58–62.

Gardner, Martin. "Mathematical Games." *Scientific American*, November 1971.

Good Housekeeping. "Never A Cross Word." June 1956, 142:21.

Graham, J.A.M. "The Right Sort of Puzzle." *Horizon*, March 1977, 19:94–95.

Grant, Annette. "*Quilty* Meets *Rebanana* in Brooklyn." *Harper's*, December 1974, 249:32–4.

Hamburger, Philip. "Onward & Upward in the Arts." *The New Yorker*, 11 December 1943, 19:62.

Hobson, L. Z. "Trade Winds." *The Saturday Review*, 22 August 1953, 36:5.

Hornaday, William. "Behold the Crossword Zoo." *Colliers*, 14 February 1925, 75:18–19.

Huston, Dorothy. "Reader's Open Forum." *Library Journal*, 15 April 1941, 66:318.

Hyers, Faith. "Editorial Forum." *Library Journal*, 15 April 1935, 60:338.

Jaquith, Priscilla. "Hardest Crossword Puzzle." *Good Housekeeping*, September 1943, 117:36–37.

James, Selwyn. "Those Crossword Puzzles." *Coronet*, March 1955, 37:115–119.

Kingsley, Elizabeth S. "Crostics Club." *Saturday Review*, 1943–46 issues.

Library Journal. "Puzzle Plague." 1 March 1941, 66:209.

Literary Digest. "Menaces to the Cross-Worders." 6 December 1924, 83:29.

———, "Why the Cross-word Puzzle?" 7 March 1925, 84:21–22.

———, "Europe at the Cross-Words." 14 March 1925, 84:32–33.

———, "Forty Resurrected Cross-Words." 6 June 1925, 85:34.

Literary Review. "Everybody's Doing It." 6 December 1924, 5:1.

Living Age. "On Anagrams." 19 December 1896, 211:822–827.

Lynd, Robert. "Cross Words." *The Living Age*, 24 January 1925, 324:216–219.

"Majolica." "When Puzzledom Was Young." *The Enigma*, August 1928.

Maleska, Eugene T. "Confessions of a Crossword Editor." *The New York Times* Sunday magazine, 28 October 1979, pp. 96–98.

McGinley, Phyllis. "Still the Most Popular Word Game (15 Letters)." *The New York Times* Sunday magazine, 20 December 1953, pp. 20–21.

The New Yorker. "Talk of the Town: Few Gnus." 13 June 1959, 35:26–27.

O'Hara, Neal. "Cross-Word Puzzles Are Only In Their Infancy." *The New York Evening World*, 4 January 1925.

Outlook. "Household Pest In 10 Letters." 24 December 1924, 138:668–669.

Pietschmann, Richard J. "Confessions of a Puzzlehead." *Travel & Leisure*, February 1977.

Poff, Mag. "The Cruciverbalists." *Roanoke Times and World News* (Va.), 15 September 1977, sect. C, pp.1–2.

Popular Mechanics. "Phaestus Disc." March 1925, pp. 408–409.

Prindle, Janice. "Eugene Maleska: The Arbiter of Down and Across." *Village Voice*, 9 May 1977, pp. 37–38.

Rachliss, Eugene. "What's a 9-Letter Word Meaning Fun?" *Colliers*, 4 March 1955, 135: 50–52.

Sherie, Fenn. "The Puzzle King: H. E. Dudeney." *Strand*, 1926, 71:398–404.

Stafford, Jean. "The Crossword Puzzle Has Gone to Hell!" *Esquire*, December 1974, pp. 144–145.

Sterne, Ashley. "The Spelling Beehive." *The Living Age*, 28 February 1925, 324:478–480.

Time Magazine. "Cross Word Barometer." 5 January 1925.

————, "New York *Graphic* Contest." 2 February 1925.

————, "Cross-Words Have Silver Anniversary." 6 August 1932.

————, "Crossword King Ximenes." 22 September 1952.

"Torquemada." "Pray You, Sir, A Word." *Fortnightly*, February 1935, 143:178–189.

Wallace, Robert. "A Man Makes a Best-Selling Game: Scrabble." *Life*, December 1953, pp. 101–102.

Warman, Christopher. "Clues to a Crossword Compiler: Adrian Bell." London *Times*, 31 July 1970.

Willig, John M. "15 Letters: Most Popular Game." *The New York Times*, 15 December 1963.

A B O U T   T H E   A U T H O R

MICHELLE ARNOT'S crossword career began in 1978, when she sold a puzzle to *The New York Times*. Since then her puzzles have also appeared in the Simon and Schuster crossword-puzzle books, *Puzzling Through 1980 with Margaret Farrar and Company*, *The Bantam Great Masters Crossword Collection* and other publications. She is the author of *Foot Notes*, a book on foot care, and her work has appeared in *Esquire*, *Glamour*, *Ladies' Home Journal* and *Travel and Leisure*. She was educated at Beloit College and Columbia University. She and her husband divide their time between New York City and Sandisfield, Massachusetts.

OTHER VINTAGE BOOKS
OF WORDS AND GAMES